New Museum of Contemporary Art, New York

the Time of Our Lives

Exhibition organized by Marcia Tucker
with Anne Ellegood

Essays by Marcia Tucker, Anja Zimmermann, Philip Koplin,
Anne Ellegood, Anne Barlow and Xochitl Dorsey

The Time of Our Lives
New Museum of Contemporary Art, New York
July 15–October 17, 1999
Organized by Marcia Tucker with Anne Ellegood

The Time of Our Lives is made possible by generous grants from The Leonard and Susan Bay Nimoy Family Foundation, The Rockefeller Foundation, and the Penny McCall Foundation.

Library of Congress Catalog Card Number: 99-70492
ISBN 0-915557-83-5

New Museum of Contemporary Art
583 Broadway
New York, NY 10012
www.newmuseum.org

Catalogue Production Manager: Melanie Franklin
Editor: Tim Yohn
Catalogue Design: Susan Evans and Brian Sisco, Sisco & Evans, New York
Printer: The Stinehour Press

Cover details: Leonardo Da Vinci, *Age Confronting Youth,* Collection of Galleria degli Uffizi, Florence, Italy. Courtesy of Ministero per i beni e le Attivita' Culturali; Susan Unterberg, *Untitled* from Father/Son series, 1990, Collection of the New School for Social Research, New York. Courtesy of the artist; Yoshiko Kanai, *In a Mirror,* 1996, Courtesy of the artist and M.Y. Art Prospects, Brooklyn; and Yvonne Rainer, Still from *Privilege,* 1990, Courtesy of Zeitgeist Films, New York.

Back cover: Alice Stone, *She Lives to Ride,* 1994, Courtesy of Women Make Movies, New York.

Inside covers, front and back: Charles J. Howard, "An Old Maid" and "An Old Cock" from *Penny Dreadful Valentines* published by McLoughlin Bros., New York. Courtesy Marcia Richards, Pitman, New Jersey.

Contents

Preface and Acknowledgments

DISCLAIMER: The fact that I decided to organize an exhibition on the topic of age has nothing to do with me personally. All artistic decisions are purely objective, and this one, I assure you, is equally so. I was, however, influenced by the fact that the *only* truly great body of artists—those born, like me, in the 1940s—are now starting to look their age.

Yvonne Rainer's film, *Privilege,* is what started it all. It came out in 1990—along with what seemed like half the audience—and premiered at New York's Film Forum. The film was shocking, not because it was Yvonne's (the art world had come to associate her work with the thoroughly unconventional), but because the word "menopause" just wasn't spoken out loud—at least, not outside the doctor's office. It's hard to believe that even as recently as 1990 the subject was still pretty much under wraps.

At that time I was not yet "past my prime," as it's so delicately put, so I had no personal experience of the subject. Of course, once enlightened, I began to see increasing numbers of works that addressed the subject of the postmenopausal body. I also saw works which dealt with the aging male body, with intergenerational issues, and with the ways that AIDS has altered the concept of age. Through all this I became painfully aware of the ageism in the visual images that surround us.

But as I looked further, it was clear that the fine arts had begun to enter into a dialogue with age theory. In academia and the social sciences, the ideas of radical gerontologists, cultural studies critics, and feminist theoreticians were upsetting the ways that age had been addressed in the past, analyzing images and offering new contexts that provided alternative ways of looking at the subject altogether.

Because works of art—in all media—are rarely literal, and because artists tend to tear stereotypes apart with their bare hands, their work can make us think about age in ways that sharply contrast with the content of standard media images. Since there was no way of covering all the issues in the field, or of even showing a "representative sampling" of the art works which address issues of age, we simply tried to include work of all kinds that turned age upside-down, contained images that were thought-provoking rather than doctrinaire, and provided a sense of what age might be like from many different perspectives.

I'd like to thank the following people, who have been instrumental in helping with the exhibition and with my sanity throughout the project:

Kathleen Woodward (54), a pioneer in the field of age studies, offered assistance, manuscripts, connections, and support from the onset. In 1996 she organized a symposium entitled "Women and Aging: Bodies, Cultures, Generations" for the Center for Twentieth-Century Studies at the University of Milwaukee, Wisconsin, which broke new ground in its exploration of issues across the fields of feminism, the visual arts, and age studies. I'm grateful to Kathleen and to Patricia Mellencamp, also at the Center, for their encouraging and enthusiastic response to this project. Through them I met Anne Davis Basting (33), who was extremely helpful with suggestions, contacts, and information about the field, and whose documentation of her work with Alzheimer's patients is included in the show. Stephen Katz (47), sociologist and author, was also gracious in providing materials and suggestions.

Cheryl Amato (49), Diana Meyers (52), and Sari Eckler Cooper (37) each generously offered their help and suggestions. Although ultimately we weren't able to incorporate their specific proposals into the exhibition, their enthusiasm and knowledge were integral to the show as it finally evolved. Other friends and cohorts, among them Estelle Berruyer, Ann Doran (42), Alison Gingerais, Melissa Goldstein (37), and Amy Fusselman (32) gave advice, made suggestions, and/or facilitated loans that were invaluable in shaping the exhibition.

My colleagues in the field, among them Carolina Ponce de Leon (43), former curator at El Museo del Barrio; Lydia Yee (32), curator at the Bronx Museum; Daniel Veneciano, former curator at The Studio Museum of Harlem; Katy Kline, Director of the Bowdoin College Museum of Art in Maine; Nancy Doll (50), Director of the Weatherspoon Art Gallery at the University of North Carolina, Greensboro; independent curator Marcia Tanner (57); Christine Taverna Reich (25), Assistant Exhibit Planner at the Museum of Science, Boston; and artist and writer Philip Koplin (56) all offered advice and suggestions that altered the final shape of the show for the better.

DISCLAIMER #2: The ages of everyone involved with the exhibition and the Museum are listed wherever possible. Where no age is indicated, we were either unable to contact the person, or there was no response. All resemblance to persons living or dead is purely coincidental.

Anita Roddick, founder of The Body Shop, Inc., has gone where no one else dared ever tread, and her enthusiasm and courage in breaking stereotypes right and left—especially those involving age and beauty—have been inspiring. Susan Bay Nimoy (56) and Leonard Nimoy (68), whose friendship can best be described as an emotional, intellectual, and artistic life-support system, not only provided funds for this exhibition but opened doors that made a crucial difference to what, how, when, and why the project came to be. I am indebted to Richard Masur at the Screen Actor's Guild and to Norman Lear for their assistance in the lengthy process of obtaining permission to use television programs. At the Rockefeller Foundation, Tomas Ybarra-Frausto's enthusiasm for the project gave it momentum and, with the help of Joan Shigekawa and Mikki Shepard, Director of the Arts Program, brought about welcome financial support. Robert Shiffler of Shastar, Inc., with the help of Kay Riffle, generously donated the furniture in the exhibition. Many dealers were extremely helpful in locating work and facilitating loans, without which there would be no show. The lenders who parted with their pieces have been particularly generous; their (temporary) loss is our—and the public's—gain.

My friends Connie Beckley (47), Kinshasha Conwill (48), Lynne Darcy (58), Ellen Diamond (59), Nancy Dwyer ("44 going on 45"), Mimi Gaudieri (58), Betty Harris (46), Maxine Hayt (62), Susana Torruella Leval (55), Patrizia Levi (60), Barbara Niblock (65), Cheryl Morrison (52), "Suzy Q." (57) and Janine Reiman (50) in New York were the linchpins that held me—and the project—together during a difficult year and a half prior to its opening. My west coast friends Marla Berns (46), Elizabeth Brown (42), Linda Cathcart (51), Arlene Dunlap (59), Meg Linton (32), Liza Lou (30), and Cissy Ross (50), were my anchors on the other side of the country; Rick (50 and 7 mos.) and Ro (47 and 5 mos.) Sanders once again provided a peaceful haven in which to research, write and relax. The wisdom of Gene Fairly (73), Martha Gallahue (60), Barry Grundlein (67), Rebecca Klinger (48), Yvonne Rand, and Dick Rifkind (69) helped me find focus and strength. My husband Dean (42) and my daughter Ruby (15) gave me themselves, which was just what I needed to see the project—and everything else—through.

At the New Museum, Greg Sholette (43), former Curator of Education, helped shape the educational component of the project in its earliest stages. Stephen Yaffe (50), who organized the professional development training series for artist instructors and high school teachers in our Visible Knowledge Program, was the catalyst for the successful collaboration which resulted in the student projects included in the exhibition. Claudia Hernandez (30), former Assistant Educator, was instrumental in conceptualizing, spearheading, and implementing the projects in 1997 and 1998. Sarah Farsad (33), Education Assistant, worked closely with Claudia and with Anne Barlow (34), Curator of Education, on just about everything. Meryl Meisler (47), an artist and multimedia teacher who was part of the collaboration, was extremely generous with ideas and suggestions for the show. It was an incredible pleasure to work with the artists, teachers, and students who contributed to the exhibition, and the results prove that high school students can produce amazing works of art in every medium.

Sefa Saglam (29), Assistant Registrar, called our attention to several unusual items that have been included in our public resource materials; she also lent her considerable skills to the installation and maintenance of the show. I am fortunate to have been able to work on this exhibition with an extraordinary group of colleagues: Melanie Franklin (32), catalogue and exhibition guru, can balance more details on the head of a pin than dancing angels, and she put it all together perfectly; John Hatfield (35) masterminded the exhibition's loans, shipping, budget, installation, and was responsible for maintaining my mental health during the process; Tom Brumley (34) juggled hammer, glue gun, paintbrush, installation crew, and harmonica with alacrity and grace; Kim Boatner (42) kept me from throwing my laptop out of the window on at least a half-dozen occasions; Dennis Szakacs capably relieved me of enormous responsibilities so that I could actually *do* the show; David Tweet's (35) fertile imagination dreamed up and commissioned age-related products for the Bookstore that would make anyone want to age instantly; Maureen Sullivan's enthusiasm and marketing mania just kept going and going and going; Anne Barlow arrived from Glasgow just in time to add fire, expertise, and the diplomatic skills of twenty to our collaborative education components; and Victoria Brown (32), cheerer-upper of the directorially distressed, resident wit, research maven, inventrix, and Genie in a Bottle™ (with unlimited wishes) also read, copy-edited, and proofed the essays, and retrieved many bits of arcane information from her secret sources.

I'm grateful to interns Danielle Jankow (24), Lara Kohl (27), Cat Marshall and Rachel Moses (35), who provided me with many pleasurable exchanges as well as the 48 pounds of invaluable Xeroxed research material that I carried with me at all times. Without the help of Anja Zimmermann (30) and Xochitl Dorsey (25) I'm not sure that I wouldn't have collapsed under the weight of such a complex undertaking—or at the very least suffered permanent eye and back strain.

Andrée Hymel (29) read the essay and offered editorial suggestions and long conversations on this and other subjects that were a breath of fresh air, as she is; Tim Yohn (59), my lifetime editor and pal, swept up the verbal debris in all of our catalogue essays, again editing with his unique combination of skill, compassion, and critical acumen. And the superb design team of Susan Evans (38) and Brian Sisco (40) once again put their talents to work to make the catalogue a genuine reflection of the show, not to mention readable. Penny McCall (1941–1999), who so generously underwrote the catalogue, was a shining example of what it means to live life to the fullest, inspiring me to write my essay in the same spirit. This exhibition is a tribute to her memory.

Above all my thanks go to Anne Ellegood (32), my partner in crime, who began to work with me on the exhibition in June 1997 and has collaborated on every aspect of it since—first as an intern studying at The Center for Curatorial Studies at Bard College, and now as a member of the Museum's curatorial staff. I'm grateful for her eye, her ear, her hand, and her heart in a project that she couldn't possibly have any interest in, given her age.

Marcia Tucker (59)
Founding Director

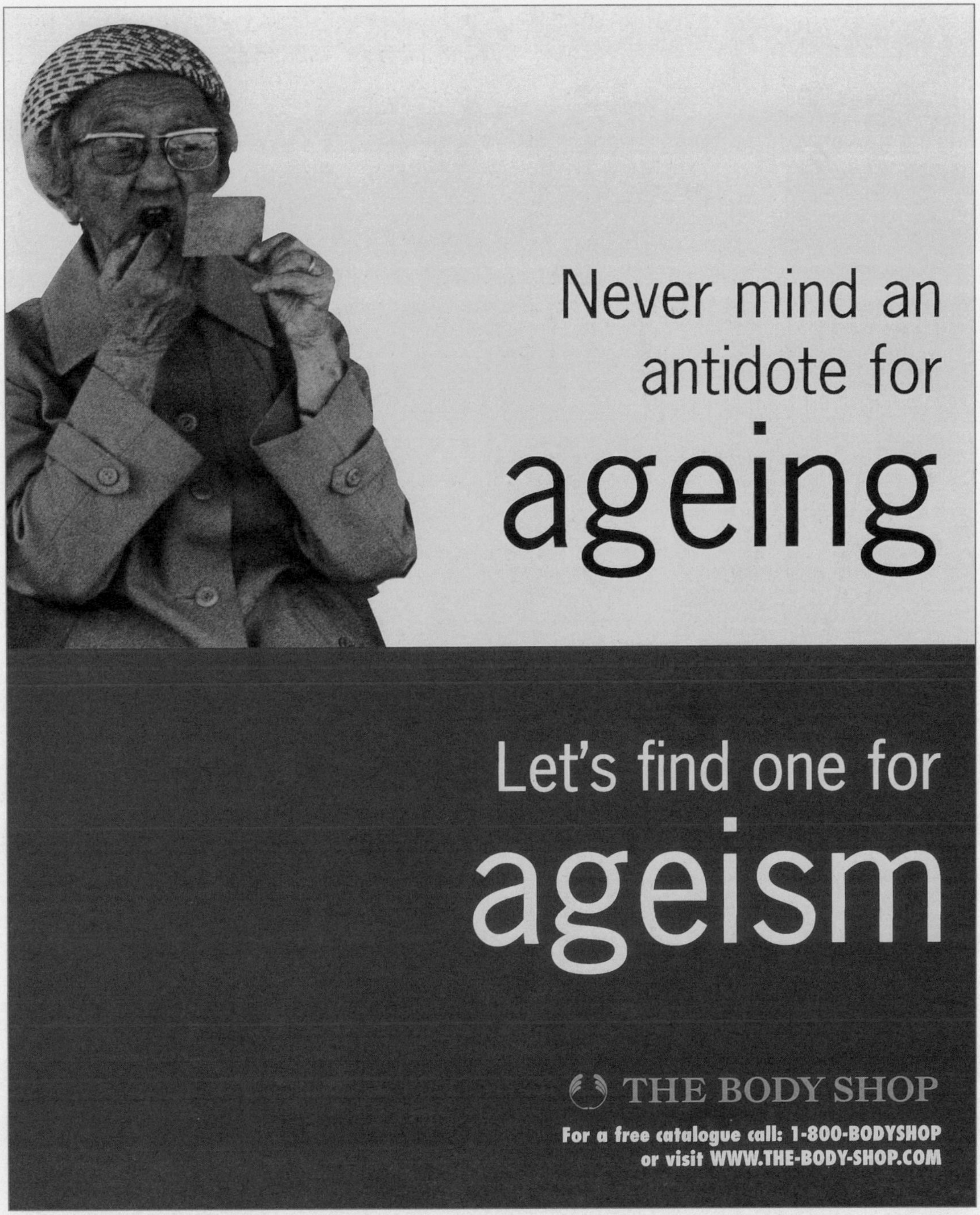

Never mind an
antidote for
ageing

Let's find one for
ageism

THE BODY SHOP

For a free catalogue call: 1-800-BODYSHOP
or visit WWW.THE-BODY-SHOP.COM

The Body Shop advertisement. *First published in* Mother Jones, *April 1999. Courtesy of The Body Shop International PLC.*

"A Land Where We'll Never Grow Old"[1]

MARCIA TUCKER

Age is a terminal disease. First you get decrepit. Your face looks like a road map with no "scenic views." Your body parts have all headed south, where it's anything but sunny. Your teeth live in a glass, except when they visit you for dinner. You've given up sex decades ago because you wouldn't want anyone to see your body; even if your parts did function you'd be asking for a heart attack or a stroke just by trying.

You can't sleep, except during dinner parties. Your hip hurts; the next thing you know, you can't walk at all. Your life is full of doctor's visits, medical bills, and insurance forms that you don't understand and can't see well enough to read anyhow. You can't remember where you put your glasses, and even if you could you wouldn't be able to see them. If someone *told* you where they were, your response would most likely be "WHAT DID YOU SAY?!!"

You're absent-minded and forgetful, which is why you put your glasses in the refrigerator in the first place. You drive very, very slowly, and badly. No one is interested in your stories except your grandchildren, and they're not all *that* interested. You go broke because Social Security has been sold to a consortium of Gen X money managers who want to use the funds as venture capital to finance a computer-controlled biological weapons center on Mars.[2] You're forced to move from your wonderful cozy apartment in Greenwich Village to a communal "retirement" complex in California, where you play bridge and Mahjong until your children send you to a nursing home, where you die.[3]

If you believe the above, you're
a) under twenty-five
b) the only child of a parent who is over sixty-five
c) a person of any age in industrialized Western culture who reads newspapers, watches TV, goes to the movies, or buys a magazine from time to time

Science proved decades ago that people don't have to lose their cognitive skills, physical or mental health, or their ability to change and grow throughout an entire lifetime.[4] So why is this picture of age still so pervasive when the facts are otherwise?

1. The title of an old hymn, which goes: "I have heard of a land/ on a faraway strand/it's a beautiful home of the soul/Built by Jesus on high/ where we never shall die/It's a land where we'll never grow old."

2. If you're well-to-do, this doesn't exactly apply. Even so, if you're a man, as all those Sugar Daddy cartoons show, once you get old, it's clear that women will only care about you for your money. If you're a woman, only the organizations who are recipients of your philanthropy will court you, much less like you.

3. My own version of the scenario, which comes from growing up in Brooklyn, the child of first-generation Jews from Russia and Poland, is that old folks never die—they just go to Miami, where they sit on the curb in the sunshine eating cat food.

4. See S. Groneck and R. D. Patterson, *Human Aging II: An Eleven-Year Biomedical and Behavioral Study*. U.S. Public Health Service Monograph (Washington, D.C.: Government Printing Office, 1971), cited in Betty Friedan, *The Fountain of Age* (New York: Simon and Schuster, 1993), pp. 72–103, passim.

In Western culture, it's not the older person but the idea of "old age" that's stuck in the mud. The "elderly"—whatever that word actually means—experience more stereotypic and prejudicial notions about themselves than any other group.[5] Age prejudice cuts across race, class, and gender, and everyone, at some point, is its target. This morning my fifteen-year-old daughter pointed out that it's the only form of prejudice that society still finds acceptable; age prejudice is not only tolerated, people don't even bother to hide their negative feelings. She also pointed out people don't seem to be fighting back; she doesn't see organized marches of old people battling for their civil liberties, carrying signs demanding the right to fair housing, benefits, medical care, employment and accurate representation in the media. (This is doubtless because they're all so sick or debilitated that they couldn't manage to get to Washington on their own, right? Tell *that* to the Gray Panthers!)

It's no wonder that we internalize the myths and stereotypes of age. People worry constantly about getting old. (Of course they also worry about being considered too young—jobs and status are denied to people on both ends of the age spectrum.[6]) But you don't find yourself bombarded daily with images that tell you that you're too young. On the other hand, the flurry of messages saying that the only role of an older person is one of increasing uselessness and incompetence will eventually get you to start thinking of yourself that way, too.[7] It's amazing to me how many "senior moments" I've experienced now that someone put a cute name to the ordinary acts of forgetfulness that everyone has. My daughter's personal conspiracy theory is that it's the great body of powerful middle-aged people who are controlling and taking advantage of those younger *and* older than themselves because, as she puts it, "they always think they know what's best."

She certainly has a point. Betty Friedan, in *The Fountain of Age,* cites recent studies showing that "midlife, rather than childhood or adolescence, represents the pivotal time of individuation, autonomous self-definition and conscious choice."[8] An article in the *New York Times* "Health and Fitness" section entitled "New Study Finds Middle Age Is Prime of Life" confirms this.[9] Despite this note of optimism, however, the article concludes, "Yet if the MacArthur study reveals mid-life as a time of relative well-being for both men and women, it also points out the risks of old age. . . . The message for people in midlife, Dr. Ryff said, is to 'be mindful of what's ahead.'" (I personally am grateful to have these risks pointed out, so I can avoid them—by suicide, say, or by catching a terminal disease, or simply by calling 1–800-GET-LOST, the Euthanasia Hotline.)

5. See *The Gerontologist* 28, no. 5, (October 1988).

6. Screenwriters in Hollywood are being denied jobs because if they're over twenty-something they're too old. Riley Weston, a writer for the Warner Brothers TV show *Felicity,* told the producers who hired her that she was nineteen. When they found out that she was actually thirty-two, they fired her as being untrustworthy. She said she lied because they simply wouldn't have hired her if they knew her true age.

7. ". . . the self-perceptions of old people are formed as responses to cultural or social definitions of age . . . [T]he human elderly, like all social beings, are embodiments of the role expectations assigned to them by their culture. In this case, the prophecy of old age as a time of uselessness and incompetence is self-fulfilling. Television does much to perpetuate this cycle." Adella Harris and Jonathan Feinberg, "Television and Aging: What You See is What You Get," *The Gerontologist* 17, no. 5 (October 1977): 467.

8. Friedan, *The Fountain of Age,* p. 113.

9. *The New York Times* (Tuesday, 16 February 1999): F6.

We figure out what "old" is from the images that surround us, and we adopt those attitudes at an early age. Try tuning in to Saturday morning cartoons sometime if you think they feature old people in a wide variety of roles; a random sampling produces the bad witch, the wicked old crone, and the evil, ancient Dr. X whose only purpose is to destroy the world.[10] So much for the broad spectrum. On prime-time TV, where the minuscule over-sixty set consists mostly of newscasters and the public figures they talk about and interview, the picture isn't much brighter. They're pretty much all guys, although there is an occasional "ageless" woman like Barbara Walters, who gets mysteriously—or not so mysteriously—younger as years go by.[11]

Sitcoms express their own particular forms of prejudice. With rare exception older people, especially female ones, tend to be the butt of jokes whenever they're shoved center stage for a moment. Business and politics, where older people are more likely to be effective and successful, aren't the stuff of which prime-time drama is made. Much more lively dramas, according to television programming, occur when people are old and sick.[12] (Of course, young and sick is even more dramatic; witness the success of *E. R.*, *Chicago Hope*, and *L.A. Doctors.*)

Several programs, however, have dealt openly with issues of age, although they were mostly comedies rather than drama. Edith's "problem," in a 1971 episode of *All in the Family*, turns out to be menopause, which precipitates a change of personality in her that is only slightly less startling than Linda Blair's in *The Exorcist*. Edith, that extraordinary embodiment of pre-feminist, cowed house-wifery, precipitously flies off the handle, refusing to accept her contemptuous, impatient husband Archie's demands. A year later, when *Maude*'s title character became pregnant at forty-seven, viewers gaped, gasped, groaned, and giggled. The second episode of "Maude's Dilemma," in which she decides *not* to have the baby, became a major topic of conversation among my friends, fresh from the trenches of first wave feminism and still torn about the reality (although not the politics) of abortion. An episode of *Cybill* entitled "When You're Hot, You're Hot" (1996) showed how much things had changed by the mid-1990s. Cybill's hot flashes unleashed a roar of appreciative laughter from men and women of all ages who admired her outspoken, unselfconscious, and hysterically funny response to the "symptoms" of menopause.[13] The long-lived (1985–92) and popular *Golden Girls* was also an exception to the rule because its lead characters were all older women, and it made age and aging a central issue, showing that older women have lives that include romance, sex, good food, meaningful conversation, and above all, friendship.[14] On the other hand, the

10. My informed source tells me that things get better once you're dead. There's a show called *Mummies Alive* wherein the embalmed dead, male and female, come to life to help fight crime.

11. See Patricia Mellencamp, *High Anxiety: Catastrophe, Scandal, Age & Comedy* (Bloomington: Indiana University Press, 1992), pp. 286–287, for a numerical analysis of the representations of older men and women in television.

12. "The areas of business and politics are rarely selected as the stage for dramatic representations. Therefore, older people who are in true life eminently successful in these fields are not portrayed in such roles in the simulated world of television entertainment. . . . Television has chosen to dramatize subject matter where old people fail (health) rather than subject matter where they succeed (business and politics)." Harris and Feinberg, "Television and Aging: What You See is What You Get," *The Gerontologist*: 466.

13. Both *Cybill* and *All in the Family* are dealt with in depth in Anja Zimmermann's essay in this catalogue.

14. *The Golden Girls* aired on NBC from September 14, 1985 to May 9, 1992, starring Bea Arthur, Betty White, Rue McClanahan, Estelle Getty, Herb Edelman, and Harold Gould.

jokes tended to enforce rather than explode stereotypes of deterioration and loss. Here's an example:

> ROSE: I don't drink before bed time. I stop all liquids at noon and I still wake up.
>
> SOPHIA: I never have that problem, never. I sleep like a log. I never get up in the middle of the night to go to the bathroom. I go in the morning. Every morning like clockwork at 7 A.M. I pee. Unfortunately, I don't wake up till 8.[15]

15. From a "Golden Girls" website.

As for age in advertising, on television everyone seems to be in a perpetual state of twenty-something grace, their lives motivated solely by the thought of a cold beer. The few commercials that aren't devoted to selling cars are promoting products for women that guarantee that they'll stay twenty-something, and products for men that will keep them in an eternal state of good old boyism—no matter how unattractive it is in real life. OK, there are exceptions. Sometimes a mother—never looking much over thirty-five—will give her adult daughter advice, usually about a feminine deodorant spray which no woman I know would ever mention in conversation, much less think of using. There's an occasional grandma who, acting like the live wire viewers know she's not, will leap, cavort, and turn super-speed cartwheels in the living room, ostensibly as proof that a battery will give new life to a dying object. Or when an older person *is* visible, he or she is reduced to an icon of that oft-touted "second childhood," the one in which our elders are seen doing the mambo across the living room in step with diapered babies and dogs, or seated at the table next to an adorable child, drooling together over the merits of a new breakfast cereal.

Occasionally, though, a commercial will so break with convention on the age-depleted screen as to appear totally shocking. An ad for IBM computers shows that older men (in this case French men who are touted as sexy at any age, unlike their American counterparts) are hardly neo-Luddites, but use the latest technology with alacrity. A McDonald's commercial shows that an older man, looking to be in his mid-seventies, is not only capable of holding down a job, but does it so well that his younger co-workers are eager to learn a thing or two from him. A while back, a Levi Strauss commercial for jeans showed a man and woman also seeming to be in their seventies. To judge by the man's interest in the jukebox-like condom machine in the corner of a seriously "rad" club, the two were about to engage in sex—yes, sex! The ad elicited some startled comments from others who saw it, like "That's just unrealistic." "They'll never sell jeans *that* way!" And perhaps most curious of all: "They're so *old,* why do they still need condoms?"

16. See Margaret Morganroth Gullette, "Midlife Discourses," in *Welcome to Middle Age! (And Other Cultural Fictions)*, ed. Richard A. Shweder (Chicago: University of Chicago Press, 1998), pp. 18–19. She has a great point to make about *Peter Pan*, which was a huge commercial success in 1904—and still is, for that matter. Wendy grows up but Peter doesn't, because she has to have babies, but he can fantasize with impunity.

17. Mellencamp, *High Anxiety*, p. 281.

18. See Gullette, "Midlife Discourses," pp. 19–22.

Last year, when a group of colleagues at the New Museum were discussing cultural differences in aging, Rika Yihua Feng commented that in China, where she comes from, if you want to sell a product you put an image of an elder with a long beard on the ad, because it implies maturity, judgment, and wisdom. In the Western world, we use a picture of a gorgeous young model in a skimpy bathing suit. What does this tell us?

As for print materials, I long ago stopped reading fashion and glamour magazines because they invariably made me feel unattractive or angry. An exception was the now-defunct magazine *Lear's*, a plank of self-esteem thrown to older female readers worried about slowly sinking into the bog of age; its pages actually showed gray-haired women, albeit mostly thin, elegant, and airbrushed, with only a few lines left in for "character." I haven't combed through *GQ* or *Esquire* lately, but I daresay that their rare images of older men are also going to be thin, airbrushed, wealthy—and white. (Admittedly, I'm not counting newspaper pictures of Boris Yeltsin, Margaret Thatcher, or Nelson Mandela in my equation, nor am I counting pictures of old folks in nursing homes, or headshots from the obituary section of the *New York Times*—which seems mostly to use pictures taken fifteen or twenty years prior to the person's death, especially if they lived a long time.) That's why a six-minute film like Gail Noonan's very funny animated video, *Your Name in Cellulite*, can blast the youth-driven attitude of mainstream media to smithereens with one good solid laugh. Isn't it odd for a society obsessed with age and aging to have so few images of people who are actually doing it?

One of the most common forms of this obsession is nostalgia, a pervasive desire to return "home" from a place of exile.[16] But alas, as the title of Thomas Wolfe's book says, "You Can't Go Home Again." (I'd love to add the subtitle ". . . Because You Can't Get There From Here.") The constant yearning for the past, for a "lost" youth, for the "good old days," starts early. My daughter was seven when she first began referring wistfully to that time way back "when I was a kid." We're taught that "young" is happy, carefree, attractive, and good. "Middle age" is the beginning of old, and old is bad. "Old" is boring, ugly, cranky, decrepit, old-fashioned, and smelly. Old is losing it.

According to cultural critic Patricia Mellencamp, in the media—as in society at large—"youth is represented as a lost object rather than a process or passage. One can imagine an acceleration of this with age, portrayed as a series of losses rather than achievements, gains, or successes for women."[17] By the early nineteenth century, men too became subject to midlife crises when they began to internalize ideas of decline and to suffer age-related anxieties,[18] particularly in

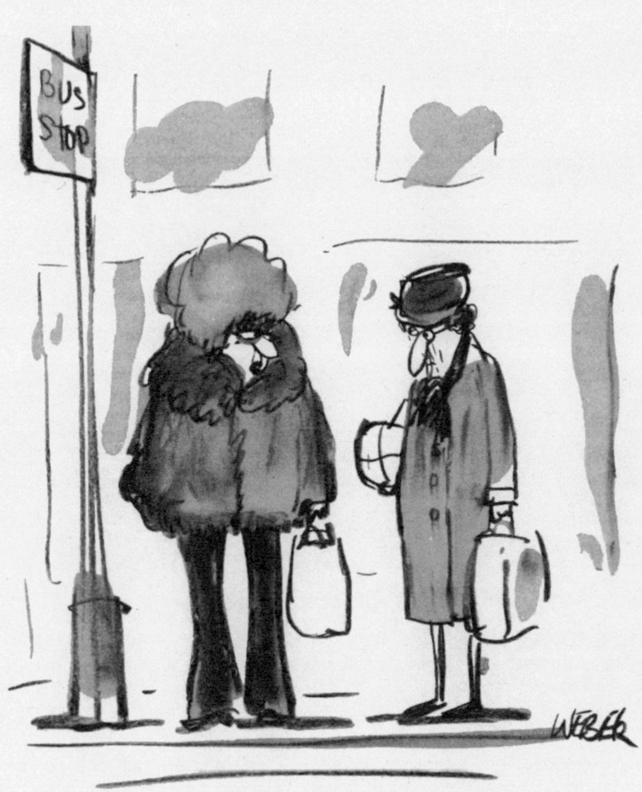

"I used to be old, too, but it wasn't my cup of tea."

relation to earning capacity, the workplace, athletic ability, or sexual performance. Even today, the images of middle-aged masculinity presented in books, plays, and popular media don't help, since most of them are hardly positive. (Witness the popularity of Arthur Miller's 1949 play, "Death of A Salesman," featuring Willy Loman, a down-in-the-mouth, down-at-the-heels Everyman, recently revived on Broadway to huge acclaim. Or the popular film *Falling Down* [1993], in which Michael Douglas [whose license plate reads "D-FENS"] goes berserk with a baseball bat, doubtless as a result of male menopause. Clearly, these guys were better off before they reached their climacteric.)

"I think your whole life shows in your face and you should be proud of that."

—Lauren Bacall

In one of the exhibition's films, *Why?,* artist Carol Halstead tells us why she went back to art school in her later life. The answer is her personal alternative to becoming a female D-FENS after her husband leaves her and their children because he says she's crazy and everything bad that could possibly happen to her does. She picks herself up, dusts herself off, and starts again. Another film, *Grace,* by Susan Cohen and William Whiteford, is a documentary love story about a woman who has Alzheimer's disease and her extraordinary husband, who cares for her throughout her illness with tenderness, compassion, patience,

19. Anne Davis Basting's workshops are included in the exhibition through handmade books, documentation, and photographs. Working associatively from a variety of visual images, participants generate extraordinary works of fiction and clearly experience enormous satisfaction in doing so.

20. Bryan S. Turner, "Aging and Identity: Some Reflections on the Somatization of the Self," in *Images of Aging: Cultural Representations of Later Life,* ed. Mike Featherstone and Andrew Wernick (London: Routledge, 1995), p. 252.

21. See Jake Harwood and Howard Giles, "'Don't Make Me Laugh': Age Representations in a Humorous Context," *Discourse and Society* 3, no. 4 (October 1992): 419.

and genuine pleasure despite the very real hardships and heartbreak of their situation. And Alain Cavalier's *Portraits*, a seven-part feature-length film about older French women at work—as a mattress-maker, a maker of artificial flowers, and the custodian of the downstairs toilets in a bar-restaurant, among others—goes a long way to dispel the myth that old women can't and don't work, especially in fields that require enormous physical strength, endless tolerance, and lost skills. It's a good example of what mainstream media are so loath to do—show the courage, common sense, hard work, and humor with which so many older people deal with the vagaries of everyday life.

Fortunately, there are other ways of looking at the passage of time than through mass media. Individual and collective memories also define the past, particularly through such oral traditions as storytelling, or narrative songs and ballads. While certainly capable of promoting nostalgia and a sense of loss, storytelling and song can also operate to subvert nostalgia and provide creative alternatives to it. A story doesn't have to be chronological, and often isn't; it weaves in and out of events and memories in an individual's life or in a given period of history. Even when a person's functional memory is eroded, as is the case with those who have Alzheimer's, their storytelling capacity may remain strong. And insofar as their tales also belie traditional chronology, they can become works of art—fictional, fluid, and shifting narratives shaped by the imagination and by personal experience—as Anne Davis Basting's workshops with institutionalized Alzheimer's patients, documented in the exhibition, so clearly prove.[19]

Nostalgia has also been aided and abetted by the advent of photography, which can record memory and measure age. Australian sociologist Bryan Turner says that "the development of the photograph has become an essential feature . . . not only of individual images of aging, but of collective, generational aging. We measure our personal aging, not simply by reference to the recorded transformation of our own image, but collectively by reference to our peers and our generation."[20] As with storytelling, though, any account can be manipulated by selecting images or historical records according to particular needs or perspectives, thereby creating subjective and varied narratives.

Nonetheless, the act of reminiscence is stereotypically considered to be the only way older people communicate,[21] implying that they live in the past rather than in the present. Since museums are the quintessential storehouses for artifacts, then, as Turner puts it, "to become old is, if there were such a verb, to be museumized." He cites Theodor Adorno's observation that the German word *museal* (museumlike) has unpleasant overtones, since it describes objects to

"The years between fifty and seventy are the hardest. You are always being asked to do things, and you are not yet decrepit enough to turn them down."

—T.S. Eliot

which the observer no longer has a vital relationship and which are in the process of dying.[22] As Turner astutely observes, aging, in our rapidly changing contemporary society, means that the meaningful cultural artifacts of a past generation are killed off and historicized by making them the subject of documentaries, remakes, and scholarly papers, as is happening with the protest generations of the 1960s and 1970s which, ironically, celebrated youthfulness. (I've experienced this personally, because my daughter considers it a loss to society as well as a personal affront that I didn't save my clothes from the 60s.)

22. Turner, "Aging and Identity," p. 253.

23. Mellencamp, *High Anxiety*, pp. 280–281.

Artists' visual representations of age challenge the assumptions of loss, irretrievability, stasis, and museumification by creating works that resist nostalgia and instead offer layered, uneasy images that defy categorization. We're used to seeing representations of the nude female body, for instance, as sexualized and objectified, but images of naked older people in the photo-based work of such artists as Jeff Wall, Consuelo Castañeda, Harriet Casdin-Silver, Jacqueline Hayden, Manabu Yamanaka, or Cindy Sherman give us embodied images of the female nude that cannot be read in a singular way. These artists have created pictorial situations in which the naked body expresses and produces a gamut of sensations and attitudes—comfortable, proud, aggressive, iconic, tender, provocative, wicked, delicate, arrogant, subversive, invincible—that offer viewers a more complex construction within which to find new dimensions and meanings for the process of aging.

Patricia Mellencamp, writing about how television images shape our feelings about age, says that "chronological age, assessed at a glance like sex, is television's and the nation's gendered obsession."[23] Chronology is pervasive, the result of living in a linear culture. But why are we so locked into this particular teleological structuring of time, when its ultimate end is cessation, or death? Even in the arts, which might have found a way around this regimentation, chronology still rules. As an artist, your life, career, and work are lined up, early to late, and valued accordingly. While chronology is a one-way street, however, value is flexible. If you're a young artist, you may get to be called a "new, hot young talent" for about 4 minutes, 38 seconds, but because your "early"

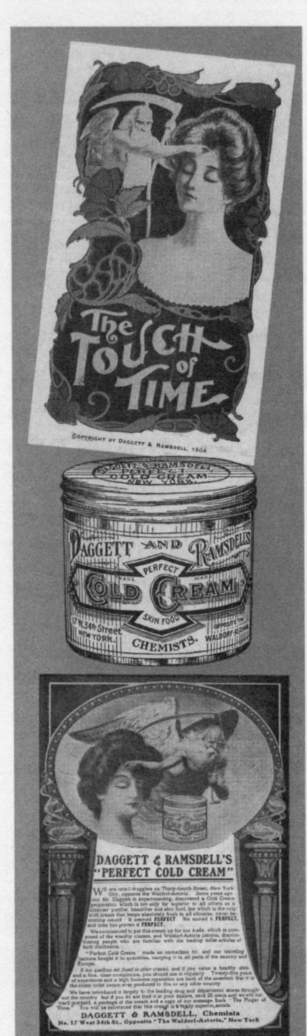

The Touch of Time. *Cosmetics ad from 1904, reprinted in 1945 edition of* Vogue Magazine. *©AM Cosmetics, New Jersey.*

work is actually quite recent it has about the same value in relation to your entire career as a starter yeast has to the bread it may eventually become. If you're a "mid-career" artist whose work has fallen out of favor with the young dealers and the old art magazines, you're referred to as someone who used to "have it" and then "lost it," expressions which invariably assign positive value to the "new" and negative value to the recent—which in this case is "old." If you're an older artist who's well-known, you may be ready for a major retrospective in which your Early, Middle, Late, and Paleolithic periods can finally be cast in concrete. If you're an older artist whose work *isn't* known, you probably have a large storage facility somewhere out in Queens. (If you're a dead artist, thank goodness, you don't have to worry about any of this.)

But the linear model is locked into almost everything we do, even when it has nothing to do with the way most cultures in the world experience life. Age-grading, which defines people by age category rather than by, say, behavior, temperament, interest, ability, character, or number of baseball cards owned,[24] is a real leader in the disempowerment field. The process starts in elementary school, and can cause long-lasting trauma if you get held back a grade.[25] Nowadays, age-defined categories include not only grades 1 through 12, but "early childhood," "childhood," "early adolescence," "adolescence," "late adolescence," "youth," "thirty-something," "adult," "middle-aged," "young-old," "old-old." For post-mortem age-grading, there's "recently deceased," "deceased," and "long dead" to look forward to. As critic and midlife theoretician Margaret Morganroth Gullette points out, this kind of classification leads to a psychological displacement in which age is blamed for virtually all one's economic, political, or social problems,[26] from joblessness to an inability to be civil to your mother-in-law.

Age isn't an exclusive, gated community of the old; it's relative, and age discrimination is pervasive from the outset. "You're too young to cross the street by yourself." "We don't want you going on dates alone until you're older." "FRESHMAN STUDENTS ARE FORBIDDEN TO HAVE VISITORS OF THE OPPOSITE SEX IN THE DORM ROOMS." "IF YOU APPEAR TO BE UNDER 26, YOU MUST SHOW PROOF OF AGE TO PURCHASE CIGARETTES OR BEER. NO EXCEPTIONS." There are laws which say that you can't drive till you're eighteen, you must be twenty-one to drink alcohol, you're not eligible for Social Security Benefits until you're sixty-two, and so on. No wonder everyone lies about their age! I did it to get into movies where minors weren't allowed, to get a job when I was sixteen, to get served in bars before I was twenty-one, and to be considered eligible by the older men of twenty-five

24. See Gullette, "Midlife Discourses," pp. 22–23.

25. My own experience was somewhat of an exception. Growing up in Bensonhurst, Brooklyn in the 1940s, I went to a junior high school where we were all more or less equal till 8th grade, when we were divided into either "RA" or "RS" classes—"Rapid Advance" or "Reform School."

26. See Gullette, "Midlife Discourses," p. 23.

who frequented those bars. On the other side of the spectrum, it came as a shock a couple of years ago to be waved through the gate at the Ventura County Fair in California without paying. I later discovered that it was "Seniors' Night," free to anyone over sixty. I was only fifty-six at the time, but they let me in without even asking for my ID!

Just as it's said that girl babies are developmentally "ahead" of boy babies, women are considered "old" at an earlier age than men. Women live longer than men—an average of nearly eight years longer—and according to recent studies seem to be more adaptable to change. In fact, the fastest-growing age group in both the United States and in the world consists of women over eighty-five.[27] And contrary to popular belief and early studies, these women do not "deteriorate" with age. The more control a woman has over her life, the less likely she is to experience any decline at all. While men are more likely to die within two years of a spouse's death, women usually go on to make major changes in their lives and to sustain themselves despite the death of their mates.[28] It's interesting to see, though, that there's been a switch in gender roles among older people in recent years.[29] Men who once brought home the bacon, often to the detriment of family life, are now rescuing babies from the bathwater with pleasure and skill, while the women who stayed home to hold down the fort are now selling it and investing the capital to sail around the world, start a new business, or organize a community garden.

Even more evident than the differences between men and women are racial and cultural differences in the conceptualization of age. For instance, what Western society considers to be the devastating, debilitating effects of Alzheimer's disease, generally requiring institutionalization, are seen as signs of an increased spiritual life in other societies. In Sierra Leone, as in Native American tribes, elders who lose the ability to speak coherently are thought to be in close communication with their ancestors—speaking to the gods, in effect—and therefore revered.[30]

For many ethnic and immigrant groups living in America and Europe, the continued role of the extended family has found three and sometimes even four generations living together, with the roles of individuals within this structure in flux, particularly in recent years. In Japan, eight out of ten Japanese over sixty-five are still living with descendants, through duty and/or custom.[31]

27. See Friedan, *The Fountain of Age*, p. 134.

28. See Ibid., p. 149.

29. See Ibid., p. 157.

30. See Jay Sokolovsky, *Growing Old in Different Societies: Cross-Cultural Perspectives* (Littleton, Mass: Copley Publishing Group, 1987), p. 166.

31. See Ibid., p. 152.

32. See Elisa Facio, *Understanding Older Chicanas: Sociological and Policy Perspectives* (Thousand Oaks Cal.: Sage Publications, Inc., 1996), p. 15.

33. See Jenny Hockey and Allison James, "Back to Our Futures: Imaging Second Childhood," in *Images of Aging*, eds. Featherstone and Wernick, p. 144.

Although the assumption is that within this extended family structure older family members are valued, there's continued evidence of the hardship placed on women in particular, especially grandmothers and even great-grandmothers who care for their children's children out of necessity. The tradition of the extended family, portrayed as a panacea for the ills of the elderly, doesn't function well in a world where poverty, crime, changes in family structure, altered life expectancy, and differing levels of education have made for major changes in society.[32] Arlene Bowman's terse film, *Navajo Talking Pictures,* explores the discrepancy between the myth and the reality of intergenerational exchange, as the filmmaker visits her grandmother at her home on the reservation. It's an uncomfortable, brutally honest examination of the lack of understanding and the irresolvable conflicts that can occur when old and new ways clash.

It's also a fact that there's a difference between being old and rich and old and poor, and the difference can amount to respect and acceptance, or repulsion and disengagement. There are overtones of gentility, refinement, even philanthropic munificence to upper-class aging, while the aged poor are tainted with the specter of the tenement, the shelter, the SRO, and the park bench. Class differences also create differences in whether older people are perceived as being attractive, since being well-dressed goes a long way to obliterating overt age discrimination. As for physical looks, only those who can afford the high costs of elective plastic surgery can be refashioned into younger-looking versions of themselves. Translated into a rock/paper/scissors game, it means that class wins over age, and age wins over race, but health wins over all—that is, depending on the kind of ailment you have and the extent of your personal resources. But outside of the privacy of your own home or the genteel seclusion of a high-end nursing facility or an environment surrounded by people who love and respect you, the not-yet-old are going to see you as the Other.

That's because in Western society, old people *are* their bodies. Defined by such physical features as incontinence, slurred speech, or immobility,[33] they're classified according to disability, rather than personality, intelligence, coping skills, or talents. Feminists who in the late 1960s and early 70s also battled against being defined by our bodies now find ourselves growing into invisibility, our physical selves no longer seen as viable. And just ahead, as all of us continue to age, we're ironically liable to find ourselves defined by our bodies once again.

This time, however, the response on the street is likely to be something other than the wolf-whistles and catcalls most women endured in their twenties and thirties. The older body is simply in bad taste, as anyone with a teenager at home

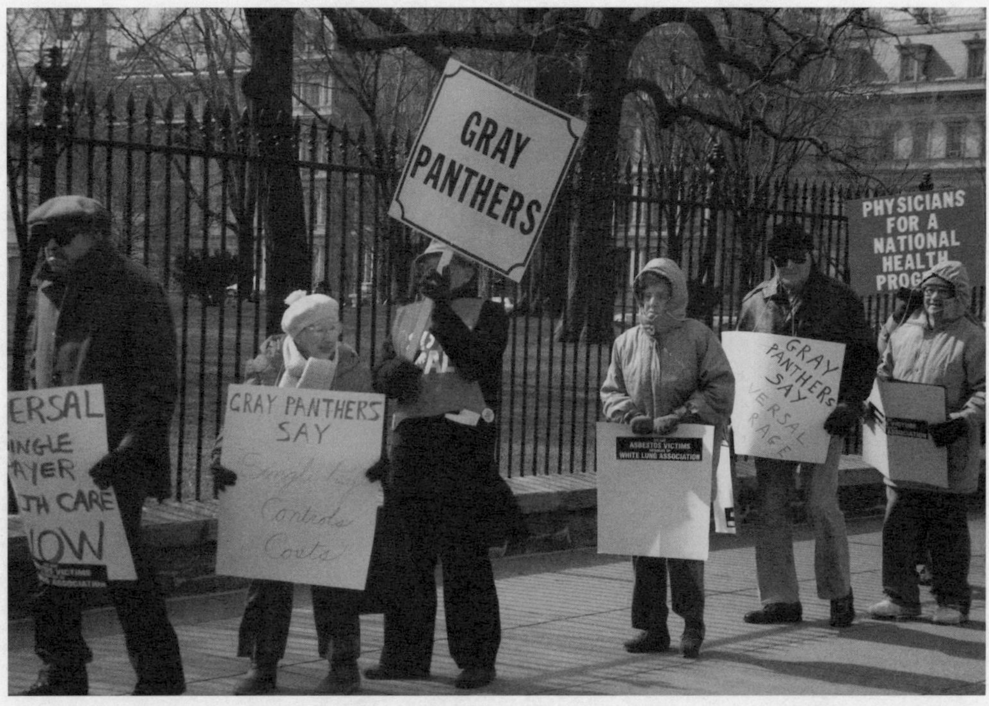

The Gray Panthers marching in Washington DC for a single-payer, universal health-care plan, March 1993. Courtesy of the Gray Panthers, Washington DC.

knows perfectly well. Its flesh is excessive (that's what wrinkles are, after all) and "unaesthetic," since what is aesthetically pleasing in bodily terms is defined by society as fresh, young, unused. Judgments of people—of all ages—on aesthetic grounds are common and usually applied to express approval or disapproval. They parallel the aesthetic judgments or properties ascribed to works of art,[34] which are no less subjective.

34. See David Novitz, *The Boundaries of Art* (Philadelphia: Temple University Press, 1992), p. 145.

Even worse than the bad taste of the aging body is what happens when that body happens to have an active sex life as well. In Liz Cane's short film *Libido* and in Heddy Honigmann's feature film *O Amor Natural*, it's clear that a sex life isn't the sole province of those under thirty-five. In these films, *much* older people are doing it, enjoying it, and talking about it. In Keiko Ibi's Academy Award winning documentary *The Personals: Improvisations on Romance in the Golden Years*, a group of actors in their seventies and older who live on Manhattan's Lower East Side are seen working on a play. Their production, and the process leading to its final form, show what it's really like to look for romance via the personal ads—especially after one is not supposed to care about such things. It seems to be in bad taste to do something about being lonely once you're too old—to be romantic, that is.

"We are all growing older from the day we are born."

—Anonymous

35. Barbara Kirshenblatt-Gimblett, *Destination Culture: Tourism, Museums, and Heritage* (Berkeley: University of California Press, 1998), p. 273.

36. Bryan S. Turner, "Aging and Identity: Some Reflections on the Somatization of the Self," in *Images of Aging*, eds. Featherstone and Wernick, p. 257.

37. Diana Dull and Candace West, "Accounting for Cosmetic Surgery: The Accomplishment of Gender," *Social Problems* 38, no. 1 (February 1991): 64.

38. Ibid., p.65.

39. On the other hand, if you look your age but refuse to dress appropriately, there'll always be someone saying "Isn't that outfit a little too young for her?" or "He's much too old to still be dressing like a hippy."

Barbara Kirshenblatt-Gimblett, writing about the culture of taste, says:

> Bad taste could be said to be bad timing. While the icons of good taste stand the test of time, the emblems of bad taste come and go. . . . These most debased of commodities are also the most fertile for recoding, because they constitute such abundant trash.[35]

She might as well be talking about the increasing numbers of "bad-tasting" older people in our society, who are, indeed, relegated to the status of debased commodity, except that no one seriously considers *them* "fertile for recoding."

No wonder Americans will do anything to avoid aging. Adapting to a pervasive societal norm by "passing" for younger is commonplace because "in a culture in which the surface of the body is seen to be that which carries the signs of one's inner moral condition, aging is something which has to be denied."[36] And there are so many ways to do it. Working out at the gym can produce or maintain a healthy, "younger-looking" body, but liposuction, breast and face lifts, collagen injections, face peels, hair and cheek implants, and dye jobs can do what even the most strenuous exercise can't. Cosmetic surgery is one of the fastest-growing industries in America, an elective that once belonged to women, but now includes rapidly increasing numbers of men.

The assumption is that it's important to look younger than you are in order to get or keep a job, find love, attract a partner, or simply be "the best that you can be." Whether you get that way through surgical alteration or by using the pervasively advertised products that purport to guarantee the look of youth, it's now considered a viable alternative to "just letting yourself go." Most people seeking cosmetic surgery don't express a desire to look younger, but instead reduce themselves to body parts which have "faults" or "defects" that they see as being in need of correction.[37] The desire for a "younger-looking" self in women, however, is accepted as natural and normal, whereas for men, who are not supposed to be anxious about their appearance, the desire for "aesthetic improvement" needs to be justified in terms of job-related or medical concerns.[38]

Pretending that aging isn't happening to you, making a distinction between "us" and "them," or adapting the styles and attitudes of the young in order to "pass," is perfectly acceptable today if you look young enough.[39] To hear people say,

"Oh, but you look so much younger than you actually are!" is considered a compliment. (After all, aren't we all the same age—about twenty-eight—inside? So why not look it?) The only problem is that the more distance you keep from your real age, the less you're able to claim its rewards, or to provide a role model for younger people by helping them to formulate less restrictive and self-destructive concepts of their own aging. Similarly, if you conceal your age because you're afraid people will think you're too young for the responsibilities you have, you lose the chance to show others that age is only one element to be considered in relation to one's abilities, skills, initiative, or commitment—and clearly not the most important one, either.

Just how much of this inevitable "deterioration" is based in biological fact, and how much is due to cultural fiction? According to scientist Leonard Hayflick, there's an enormous difference between the biological and the medical aspects of old age; biological aging considers what is normal, whereas medical aging deals with abnormalities.[40] While the passage of time can be quantifiably measured, biological age can't be easily defined because not enough is known yet about the many biological clocks that regulate the aging process.[41] Hayflick says that only two of them, the chemical clock called melatonin and the cell division that causes the tips of each of our cells' forty-six chromosomes, called telomeres, to shorten, have been studied in enough depth to provide adequate information.[42] According to him you're as old as your oldest cells, the neurons and skeletal muscle cells you were born with and still have because they don't divide or turn over.[43] Under any circumstances, Hayflick and others assure us, *all* aging is normal aging, no matter how "old" you look—or think you do.[44] So, biology may not be destiny after all.

There are, of course, normal physical and psychological changes that occur more often as we age and it's important to acknowledge and address them. Would you, after all, want to give up reading just because your eyesight changes in your forties? By addressing changes in physical aptitude, health, job status, relationships, roles, and interests at every age, we're more likely to discover different aspects of ourselves as we adjust and compensate for those changes.

The film and video pieces in *The Time of Our Lives* deal with age across a broad spectrum of feeling and experience. Many are intergenerational, showing the frustrations of communication between, say, father and son, as in Alan Berliner's *Nobody's Business,* or the enormous pleasures accorded to both parties when older singers are paired with their secondary school counterparts, as is so movingly shown in Nigel Nobel's documentary film *Close Harmony.* Older people are portrayed in every conceivable situation, from the bronco-busting and

40. See Leonard Hayflick, *How and Why We Age* (New York: Ballantine Books, 1994, 96), p. xix.

41. See Ibid., p. 13.

42. Ibid., p. xxi. (I was surprised to learn that the only "immortal" cells in our body are cancer cells, which are distinguished by telomerase. Does this put a good spin on a bad disease?)

43. See Ibid., pp. 16–17.

44. Ibid., p. 43. There is a condition called Progeria (Hutchinson-Gilford syndrome), a rare genetic disease that accelerates the aging process from infancy to death by about age 13, but death is usually caused by a stroke or heart attack rather than as a result of aging itself. Nancy Burson's work in the exhibition addresses this painful subject.

"*The hardest years in life are those between ten and seventy.*"

—Helen Hayes, at age 83

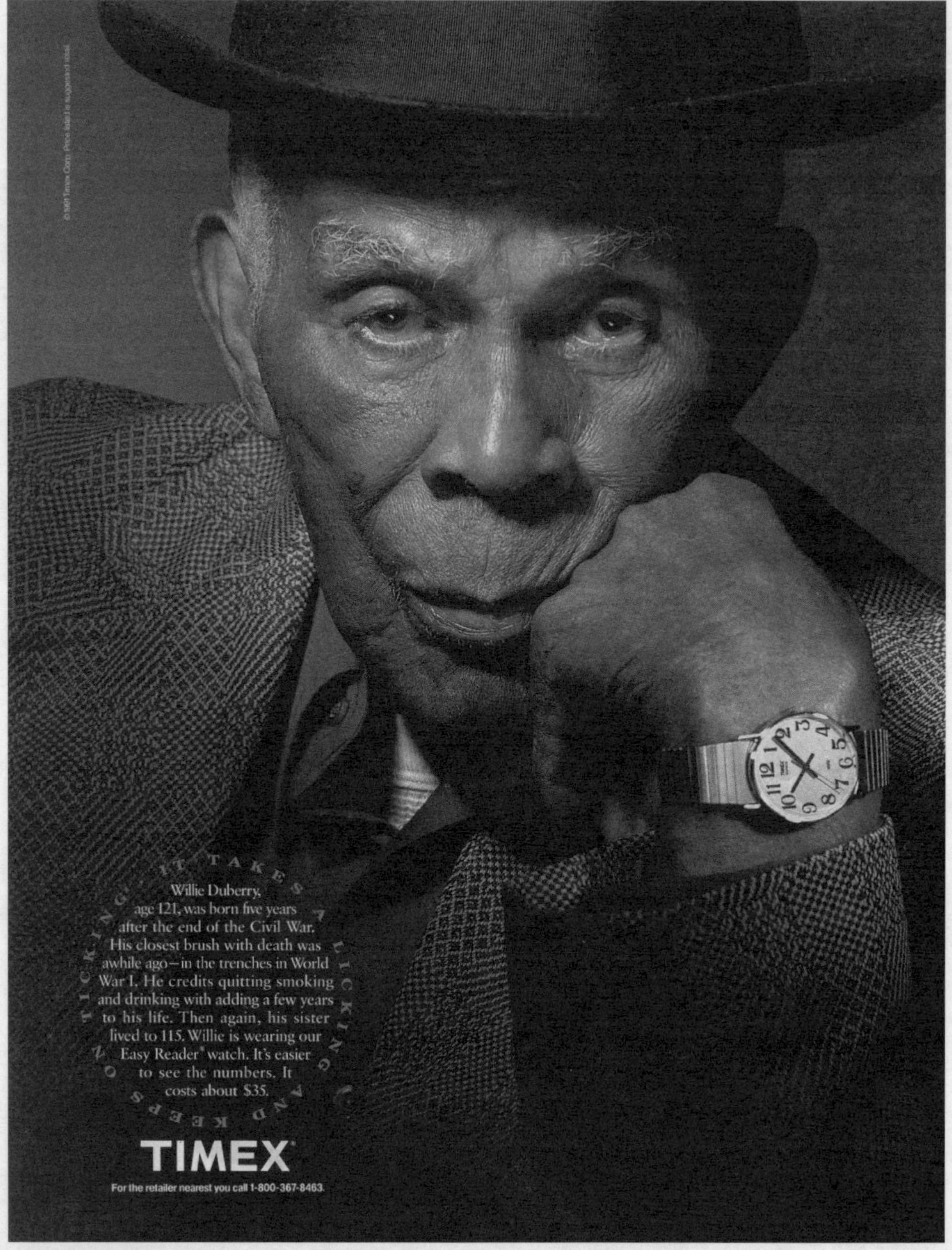

Timex advertisement.
Published in Newsweek*, November 4, 1991. Photograph of Wille Duberry at age 121. ©1991 Timex Corporation. Photo: Hiro.*

motorcycle-riding women in Amanda Micheli's *Just for the Ride: Bucking Convention, Cowgirl Style* and Alice Stone's *She Lives to Ride*. The Yiddish folk-singers who gather daily at a park in Miami Beach to teach each other traditional songs, as documented by Joel Saxe; the generations of Swedish women in Kiti Luostarinen's *Gracious Curves*, enjoying their bodies as they swim together; the older lesbians of Lucy Winer's *Golden Threads* honoring a beloved role model; the differences in how younger and older gay men feel about age that are explored in Johnny Symon's *Beauty Before Age*—all show that age is just what it is, as varied as everything else in life.

Betty Friedan challenges the chronological construction of our lives when she speculates that the years after fifty might offer an additional stage of growth and development rather than a steady regression back to the helplessness of infancy:

> If one applies to age the new knowledge of the non-linear, dynamic nature of development—of the brain, the biological organism, and of the self—it becomes clear that development can continue, with losses, gains, reorganization, depending on what one's environment permits and what one chooses to do. Indeed, it now appears that the traditional linear model is no longer valid even for studying childhood development. Recent research shows that development in childhood is characterized not just by gain, and does not consist of a mere cumulative layering of stages, but at each stage brings a dynamic reorganization.[45]

Friedan also makes reference to the Jungian concept of age as a paradigm shift, a creative "rebirth" in which "living itself becomes the point."[46] Like Zen practice, in which the idea of a fixed self can dissolve into an infinite concept of being, letting go (of the familiar, of the known, of the defined self) can help us, paradoxically, to become more connected, open, generous, and creative. It would seem, in this model, that the only constant is change. If life is programmed to evolve along a linear path, toward a specific series of goals, it's harder to accept changes, especially those you haven't allowed for. Those who see their lives as open-ended, multiple, and flexible at any age are more apt to focus on the process of living rather than on its product—which, in a way, can only be death.

So it is with artists, whose work may be influenced by, but doesn't depend on, external circumstance. Artists adapt themselves continuously to change, even precipitating it when it's just too calm for comfort. Performance, film, and video artists commonly employ nonlinear narratives using time, space, and language to create open-ended, shifting, and fluid stories whose meaning depends on the

45. Friedan, *The Fountain of Age*, p. 114.

46. Ibid., p. 466.

47. Hayflick, *How and Why We Age*, pp. 57–59.

48. Friedan, *The Fountain of Age*, p. 129.

49. Thomas R. Cole, *The Journey of Life: A Cultural History of Aging in America* (Cambridge: Cambridge University Press, 1992), p. xxi.

relationship of viewers to the work and the context in which they're viewed. Films by Yvonne Rainer, Agnes Varda, or Jacob Young, for example, encourage or create multiple, layered perspectives for viewers, no two of whom seem to have seen the same film, so varied are the viewers' responses.

One could easily show that the process of aging, like the process of art making at its best, involves a sense of risk, adventure, connection, and engagement with the world around us. At least it does for most of the artists I've known and worked with over the past thirty years, and for most of the older people I've known, including myself. It takes courage to live the life of an artist, just as it takes courage to accept and enjoy one's age, whatever it may be.

There are more middle-aged and older Americans today than there are younger citizens. In the year 2000 there will be between 32 and 38 million people over age sixty-five. Of these, more than 6 million will be over eighty-five (barring wars, natural catastrophes, plagues, etc.). The only age group that will experience a significant increase in numbers in the twenty-first century, given present birth rates and immigration patterns, will be people over age fifty-five.[47] The figures are similar in Europe. This is the first time "men and women now alive can expect a vital third to half of life after they have reproduced."[48]

Does this ring your alarm bells? Does it make you feel gleeful? Do you think things are better because the population of those over sixty-five has tripled since 1900? What age do you think is "old," anyhow? The historian Thomas Cole, in *The Journey of Life*, says that gerontology, like so many other scientific fields, has traditionally cut ideas, images, and attitudes loose from the "facts" of aging; it has made age an abstraction by denying that our beliefs and feelings about it have any basis in fact, or any role in determining how we actually do age.[49]

"Old age is like climbing a mountain.
You climb from ledge to ledge. The higher you get,
the more tired and breathless you become,
but your view becomes much more extensive."
—Ingmar Bergman

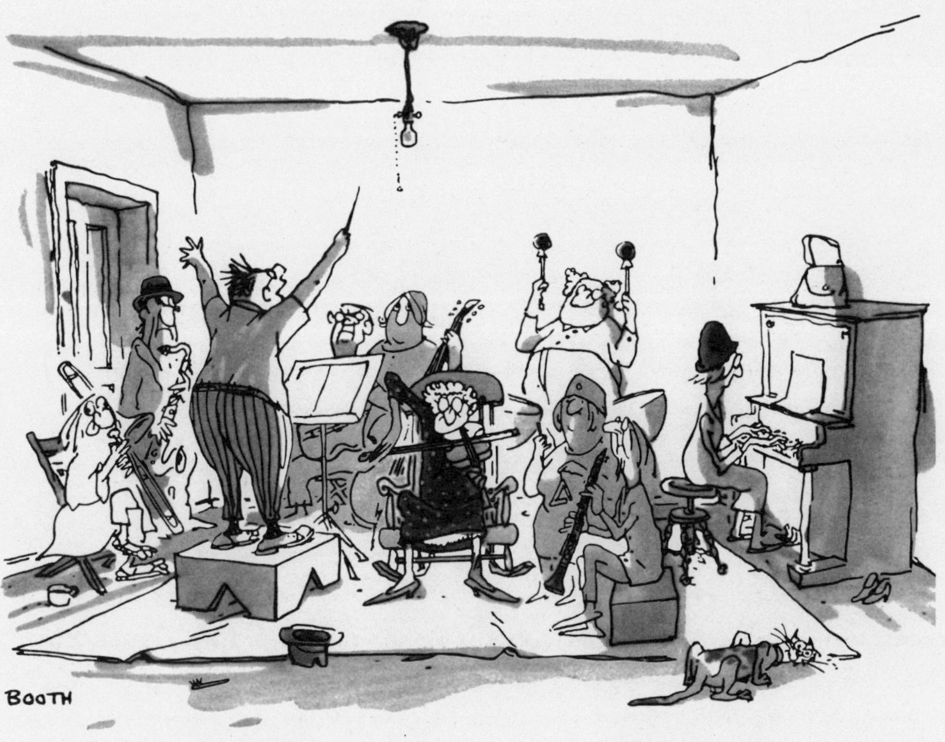

"From the top—'Watermelon Man.' Let's sock it out and give Mrs. Ritterhouse a chance to really cook!"

George Booth.

But new work in age studies, across many disciplines, has proven otherwise. Experiential, psychological, emotional, and spiritual factors far outweigh the "facts" of scientific aging, which for so many years were based on studies with institutionalized older white men, rather than long-term, broadly based studies of older people of all kinds.[50] Now that we are beginning to see the results of the longitudinal studies, as well as a marked change in the demographic distribution of age, it's time to look again. It may very well be that those giant hordes of elders swarming over the horizon at the century's end will help us to revise our ideas about what aging was, is, and can be.

50. Sokolovsky, *Growing Old in Different Societies*, p. 166.

Maybe it's time to acknowledge the fact that aging won't kill you, that it's not a disease, and that it's a normal process in our lives—*all* of our lives, *if* we're lucky. When you think about people who are all too happy to get old, they're often those who belong to cultures where chronological age is irrelevant or revered. In the West, it seems that people who are at ease with age are either lifelong Zen practitioners or people who want to experience every aspect of each age of their lives fully. Among those who want to get older are people living with AIDS, cancer, or other life-threatening illnesses, Holocaust

51. Friedan, *The Fountain of Age*, p. 72.

52. See Cole, *The Journey of Life*, p. xxviii.

53. Cited in Kirshenblatt-Gimblett, *Destination Culture*, pp. 274–275.

survivors, who are the last living witnesses to an event too terrible to believe on paper alone, or those who, not having been blessed with traditional "good looks" when they were young, gain agency as they age. Clearly, there is enormous range and diversity in how people age, how they feel about it, and how they express those feelings.

For most of our adult lives, we're valued for what we do; with age, we can move instead toward being valued (and valuing ourselves) for who we are. The concept of age has at last come to a place where we can see it as "a state of becoming and being, not merely as ending."[51] As the numbers of older people rapidly increase, it's possible that we're moving away from the idea that biology is destiny. Age, like culture itself, isn't the story of progress but is an open-ended development with no end in sight.[52]

This essay is dedicated to the memory of my mother and father, Dorothy Wald Silverman and Emmanuel Silverman, who never had the chance to grow old.

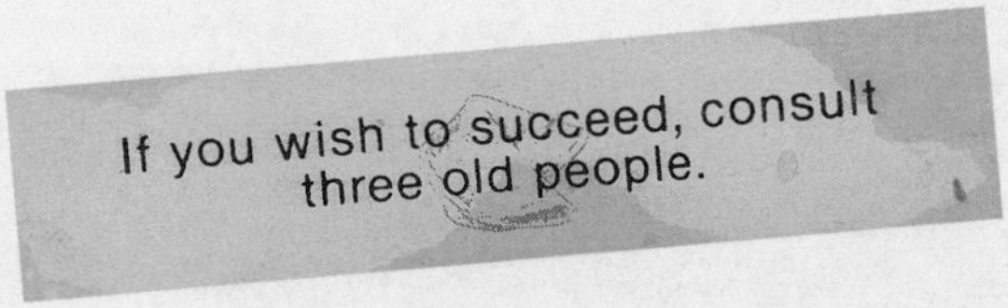

Walter Benjamin points out that the outmoded is a source of revolutionary energy because to pick it up again once it has been discarded is a potentially radical gesture.[53] This idea, when applied to aging, is a particularly seductive one. I can see it now—older people joining forces with younger generations as friends and colleagues, offering each other examples of what it's like to be independent, outspoken, and fearless. The result would be to rebel, to dismantle the definitions, institutions, and practices that keep us from ourselves, and from each other.

If you wish to succeed, consult three old people.

Marcia Tucker's fortune cookie, 1997.

Diary and Journal Excerpts
1955–1999

January 8, 1955: *"Today I went to Grandma's with the family—she's 88, and we had a birthday party at the nursing home. I don't enjoy going there very much, because it's so morbid. And I don't like Aunt S. She's getting old—wrinkles and bags and an old crank."*

January 10, 1956: *"I went to see the Rabbi this afternoon. He answered my questions about my purpose in life and whether or not there was an afterlife. He says we should live this life and work toward making others happy, and when we fulfill our purpose then we won't be afraid to die. That seems like logical reasoning, and I don't have to believe in an afterlife if I don't want to."*

April 10, 1958: *"What I want:*
1. Want to be loved
2. Want to be famous
3. Want to travel
4. Afraid of death
Remember, dear world, I am still a child of seventeen, at least until Friday. Then I stop being jail bait, can drink in the city. Amen."

July 2, 1958: *"I read over my 11th grade diary and almost cried, it was so pitiful. Every page began with 'met a really* cute *boy today.' And as I read it over I thought about how young and silly and fickle it was."*

April 10, 1959: *"this is the last time i'll be a teenager. now i am tired and hungry and beer-sogged, my hair is falling in my eyes and god i want to sleep. but no, first i must reflect upon being 19, first i must add tears to the stale beer and lament my friendless condition. i am lonely and itchy and nothing in the world satisfies me because i am such a fool in my uniquely obnoxious way. i am not really lost although i like to think i am. b. tells me that living is just a little piece of all living, that suffering is just a little piece of all suffering, that dying is just a little piece of all dying, and that i have not learned my lesson. i think i'll go to bed."*

May 1, 1959: *"I talked to Dad when I came home, and he understood what I was trying to say. He started to cry. He bought me a pack of cigarettes. He said that it was as if he were reliving his childhood again."*

January 19, 1963: *"Wedding is over and done with. Had three swift martinis upon entering reception and felt much better. Things are tranquil now, but they are bound to change—as I get older I become more moralistic (remembering that I am an ancient 22 years old) but have the erstwhile title of 'Mrs.,' something I never really wanted in the first place."*

December 28, 1964: *"I am a grown woman and I have nothing but mediocrity behind me, and probably in front of me. The horrible thing is that I will cease to be tortured by this fact as I grow older, and the tides of complacency will wash me out to sea."*

October 20, 1965: *"Feelings that I cannot possibly do anything but die—what other possibility is there? I can't envision myself as an old woman, because the only way I could bear it would be to have a family and the things which not only comfort one when age creeps up, but which in a sense give one a reason for growing old."*

January 1, 1967: *"Moments of growing older—usual feminine narcissism—lines, flab . . . probably a manifestation of self-hatred in its most elementary form."*

August 26, 1967: *"I'm frightened of getting old—I would very much like to change that into curiosity. Therefore from now on I'll try to record (like a movie of a plant blossoming, ripening and dying) the change in features as I age, by taking pictures every month."*

October 4, 1968: *"Had a party tonight because I've just become a museum curator. All of a sudden, everyone listens to you, which makes it harder to keep working, changing, growing. I don't ever want to try to maintain the status quo in my life or my head or my actions. Instant middle age and atrophy."*

December 28, 1973: *"Fear of living alone, fear of the dark, fear of growing old, of not being able to write well, of having no one to talk to."*

April 13, 1975: *"Just had my 35th birthday, and who ever thought I'd ever be 35? Certainly not me. Look older—have short hair. Haven't grown up at all. My body betrays me. It ages, I don't."*

April 15, 1975: *"My mother began to die when she was 38; I realize that I am waiting for that time, since I too will begin to die then."*

September 20, 1976: *"I'm obsessed with growing old, becoming middle-aged, ill, eccentric, unloved, unwanted, frightened, in pain. And I'm 36, at my best personally and professionally (sounds like a letter of recommendation) and consumed by uncertainty and self-doubt."*

July 12, 1979: *"Yesterday, in the canoe by the lily pads, I felt an incredible, overwhelming sense of the ephemeral—how nothing could ever be maintained, preserved, captured."*

April 11, 1980: *"Big day. I'm forty. Never thought I'd live this long. I feel very much my age; I keep thinking of a 'ruined' face. I look so old. Even though I never thought I'd live this long, I wonder exactly* how *I'm living."*

December 27, 1981: *"The willingness to—no, the intense and addictive pleasure resulting from—changing one's mind is sometimes all that counts."*

March 18, 1982: *"I'm going to be 43 next month, and even if I could have a kid now, would I want to? How much more can I do?"*

July 18, 1983: *"We got married yesterday... Here I am, more than halfway through my life, and I'm* having fun*—who would have thought?"*

January 18, 1984: *"I can't believe I'm a Mom!!! This is the BEST!!! ..."*

September 22, 1986: *"For 25 years, I've tried to understand others and to 'interpret' through their eyes. Suddenly it strikes me—that makes 25 years of trying to avoid the painful process of looking into myself."*

August 26, 1989: *"My life is going by very, very fast, and I'm afraid of being so busy/worried/frustrated/overworked that I don't live it. Next year I'll be fifty, and as far as I'm concerned, I haven't grown up* yet. *And probably won't ever."*

April 15, 1990: *"Well, I've finally made it to the big one! And except for seeing my face and body age, I've never felt better, more productive, more effective, stronger, happier, or more loved."*

July 20, 1993: *"Aging—real aging—is a painful process. It's hard not to note that I've always been aware of it (or at least since I saw that first wrinkle in the mirror when I was, what? 30?). The advantage to visible age, on the other hand, is what I call the Unedited Mouth. It means that you can go anywhere and be as outspoken, outrageous, funny and/or controversial as you want to be, and people will actually pay attention."*

June 19, 1995: *"I really am zooming down the path of age, more of my life behind me than ahead. It's maddening because you can't control it. I realize that all the other things I was going to do or be someday when I grew up I probably won't do or be."*

March 11, 1996: *"Yvonne Rand, the Zen master, says that we have to take care of our relationship with ourselves, because our capacity for our relationship with others is dependent on it."*

October 25, 1998: *"This is going to be an extraordinary time, if I let it be. Trying to come to terms with who I am isn't easy after a lifetime of trying to be whoever and whatever anyone else needs me to be."*

***Thomas R. Cole,* The Journey of Life: A Cultural History of Aging in America**
(Cambridge: Cambridge University Press, 1992), pp. xxx–xxxiii.

Every society creates symbols, images, and rituals that help people live meaningfully within the limits of human existence. Meanings of aging and old age are inevitably linked to these cultural forms that symbolize life's meaning. And such cultural representations of life's meaning finally involve some intuitive grasp of its wholeness or unity. Until recently, Western culture has relied on two archetypal images to represent intuitions of the wholeness or unity of life—the division of life into ages (or stages) and the metaphor of life as a journey. These fundamental images, therefore, are the essential cultural forms for the history of the meaning of aging.

Classical antiquity first connected the ages of life and the journey of life, weaving them into its beliefs about the nature of human existence and the cosmos. In the Middle Ages, Christian writers adopted Greco-Roman ideas about the ages of life and conceived of the journey of life as a sacred pilgrimage. From the Reformation, which forged modern imagery of the life cycle, until World War I, which hastened its demise, various combinations of these images provided an existentially vital and culturally power framework that helped sustain the meaning of aging and old age in middle-class culture.

The archetypal power of these images derives from their capacity to help us approach the mystery of human temporality. Virtually universal, they appear in many cultures not as cognitive abstractions but as ritualized elements of individual and social life. Each offers a way of conceiving fragmented, sometimes chaotic, ever-changing "life time" as a unified whole. This imagined whole, within which various parts of life can be located, guarantees a coherent (and not always happy) place for aging and old age.

By the fifth century B.C.E. Greek legend and custom had divided human life into three ages, each corresponding to a generation, each possessing its own set of natural characteristics and prescribed behavior. Aristotle formalized this threefold division in the *Rhetoric,* where he discussed the ages of growth, stasis, and decline. Hippocrates described four physiologically determined ages—the most common scheme until the late Middle Ages, when the astrologically based system of seven ages was translated into the vernacular and eventually immortalized by Shakespeare's cynical Jacques:

> All the world's a stage,
> And all the men and women merely players.
> They have their exits and entrances;
> And one man in his time plays many parts,
> His acts being seven ages.
> *As You Like It,* act 2, scene 7

In *De Senectute,* Cicero identified the philosophical bedrock beneath the ages-of-life conception—the belief that despite the diversity of size, appearance, ability, and behavior that characterizes the different ages, the human lifespan constitutes a single natural order. "Life's racecourse is fixed," wrote Cicero, "nature has only a single path and that path is run but once, and to each stage of existence has been allotted its appropriate quality."

The ages of life offers a broadly unified view of a human lifetime; the processes of birth, growth, maturity, decay and death appear as parts of the cycle of organic life. But growing up and old is not only a *process,* rooted in our biological existence, structured by social and historical circumstances. It is also an *experience,* an incalculable series of events, moments, and acts lived by an individual person. This experience, this passage through the maze of the inner life, has been traditionally represented by the journey of life—a metaphor that operates by narrating diverse experiences in time and space, bringing them under control of a single unifying purpose.

... Although both the ages motif and the journey motif offer images of life as a whole, each leaves out the other's essential insight. The ages of life envisions the biologically and socially structured process of the human life cycle. The journey of life emphasizes the fluid and unique qualities of individual experience, the spiritual drama of the traveler's search. A deeper understanding of human "life time" requires some imaginative fusion of the two themes, in which neither is reduced to the other and both together create a whole greater than the sum of their parts. Existentially adequate and culturally powerful meanings of aging emerge when artists, writers, theologians, philosophers, or scientists hold these two motifs together in creative tension and weave them into their culture's view of the relations between cosmos, society, and self.

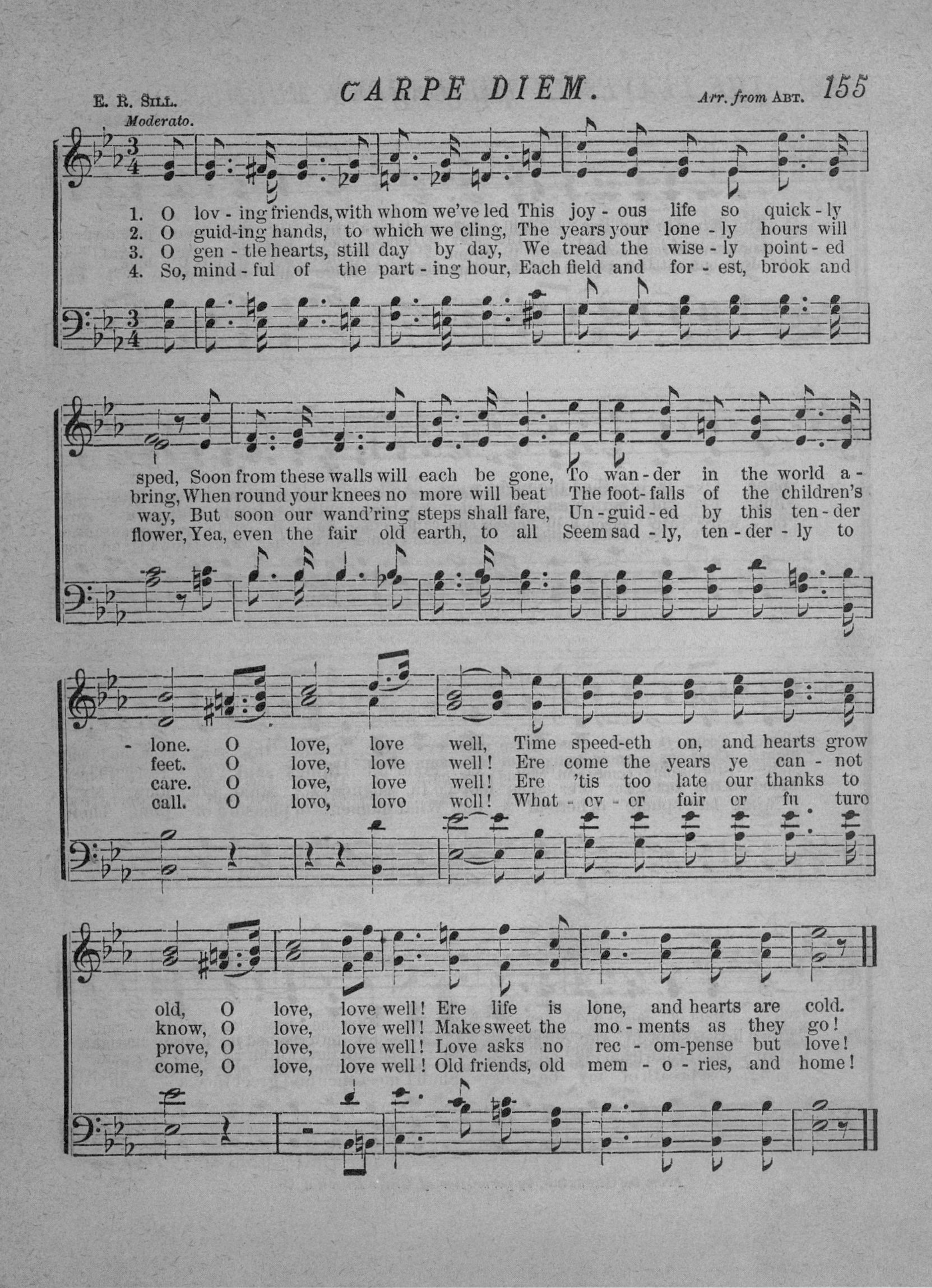

33

Reproduced from E.R. Sill,
The Song Sheaf *(Boston and New York: Taintor Brothers and Company, ca. 1884), p. 155.*

***Mike Featherstone and Andrew Wernick, eds.,* Images of Aging: Cultural Representations of Later Life** *(London: Routledge, 1995), pp. 2–4.*

Given [the] problem of translating experience across generations to human beings who are generally preoccupied with the view of the world from their particular juncture in the life course, we often have to resort to literary and artistic forms, to novels, poetry, films and other modes to get a sense of meaning of old age. Here we think of the grim depictions of the aging body, the preoccupation with memory, the past and impending death, in Thomas Mann's *Death in Venice* or Patrick White's *The Eye of the Storm*.... It is from the humanities, then, that we find attempts to grapple with the meaning of the aging process.... Such research points to the way in which the aging body is never just a body subjected to the imperatives of cellular and organic decline, for as it moves through life it is continuously being inscribed and reinscribed with cultural meanings.

To highlight the importance of the body for the study of aging, then, is not to raise the spectre of biologism, the reduction of culture to the biological, nor is it to vaunt a social constructionism in which the body is conceived as a blank slate on which culture can write at will. There are strong culturalist accounts of the religious compensations the elderly can enjoy, which emphasize the way people went happily to death confident in the certainties of a cosmology which made this ultimate life transition seem a mere step towards a better life.... Yet it is hard to take such accounts of the happy death at the end of a fulfilled life as the complete story, given the existence of other accounts which focus more on the body politics of everyday life, on the power deficit and threat of violence experienced by those whose bodies weaken and do not work well.... The capacity to re-code the body itself is part of a historical process in which the religious capacity to give significance to aging, old age and death, is itself subject to change, not merely through shifts in modes of cultural classification, but also through the way a particular form of knowledge through biomedical and information technology has increasingly developed the capacity to alter not just the meaning, but the very material infrastructure of the body. Bodies can be reshaped, remade, fused with machines, empowered through technological devices and extensions. The current significance of the aging body has to be understood at a point in history at which there are strong claims that the capacity to crack the code of the human aging process is about to be achieved.

It is here we encounter the problem of the relationship between culture and the body. Because the body has material presence, its very tangibility and visibility as it moves through the everyday world of practical actions seem to suggest that we know what we see. Likewise with images of the body. They seem to possess a high degree of realism and indexicality; as if the body is something which has slipped under the guard of discourse and the process of representation to the extent that bodies are things which are self-evidently what they seem to be.... There is then, the tendency to see the body as something which can easily be copied or represented—as in the case of a photograph which is often seen as an accurate record of the way a person looked at a particular moment in time. This aspect, the notion of copying and producing an accurate likeness of the original, is one of the meanings of the term image which can be traced back to the original Latin meaning of the term imago....

The term image has, however, a second aspect, referring to imagination—emphasis is more on distortion and refashioning, on refraction as opposed to reflection. Anyone who has looked at a photograph of themselves has doubtless discovered this second aspect to making an image. For it is rare that we feel that the photographer has produced an adequate rendition of our selves—the assumption being that a good photographer is one who artfully arranges and waits for what they take to be a particular apt expression of ourselves, manifest in our face, appearance and posture, which lets the self somehow shine through. This second sense steers us away from the notion of documentary evidence, to one of the original sense of photography: painting with light. It suggests that the making of an image is an interpretative act in which the subject's body is clothed and adorned in particular ways and framed in a setting of other material objects, all of which carry a particular symbolic weight, emotional tone and resonance.

The image is, then, the result of an act of perception and construction which frames a world. Yet the artful construction of an image should not be taken to imply that its meaning is a self-evident product of its construction. The meaning of the image gains its resonance in the practices and ways in which it is viewed, in the discourses and ceremonial rituals which surrounded its use. As a photograph relates to a specific point in the lifetime of a person and their relations to other persons at that time, it carries a hidden significance and emotional charge which are themselves unstable, altering with the changing vicissitudes of their subsequent lives. It is the openness to the sense of loss of the substance of one's own body and face with all it might have been able to represent: the sense of discrepancy between one's self-image and the image we take others to see, and their subsequent dialectical interplay, which envelops photographs with poignancy and the potential for nostalgia, once we reach 'a certain age.'

Studs Terkel, Coming of Age: The Story of Our Century By Those Who've Lived It

(New York: The New Press, 1995).

Valerie Taylor, 79, Tucson, Arizona. pp. 313–314.

I talk to kids in high school and they always come up with this question: "Do you think it's fair to take social security, 'cause there isn't gonna be any left when I get there?" My answer is: "Yeah, I don't think it's fair. But just what are you going to do with your old grandmother? You can either let her starve or put her on social security. Or you can take her out and shoot her, so you'll be sure to have some money yourself when you're older." The kids looked shocked. Especially the Hispanic kids, who are very grandparents-oriented. Tucson is about 30 percent Chicano. I find the Chicanos are, as a rule, kinder, more courteous, and more civilized than most Anglos.

... Some things are very much the same now as then. Family relationships don't really change that much, although I have an unmarried twenty-seven-year-old friend who just had a baby. She's a lesbian and doesn't have a regular lover. A lot of lesbians have babies. You can get artificial insemination. In some cases, my lesbian friends have chosen a father for the baby. Usually, a good guy who will not intrude upon them, but who will hold himself responsible. I'm in favor of it. If a woman wants a baby, why shouldn't she have one.

What changes a great deal is the attitude toward age. When my grandmother, the camp-meeting Methodist, was forty years old, she stopped wearing hats. She wore a bonnet. At forty, she was too old to wear a hat. It was just before the turn of the century.

After Grandpa died, she came and lived with us. She was about seventy-six. We got her into colored clothes. She's been wearing black and gray all these years, little old bunched-up black dresses. My sister took her out and bought her a straw hat, like a pie plate, the style in 1928. It has a little wreath of pink flowers around it. Grandma fell in love with that hat. She insisted on going to church so she'd have some place to wear it. She took a whole new lease on life and lived to be eighty-four. She made a splash. The idea of who's old and who isn't has changed.

Aki Kurose, approaching 70, Seattle, Washington. p. 55.

Around 1965, I was a Head Start volunteer. I got turned on to working with young people, so after my children were raised, I went back to school. I got my master's degree in early childhood education when I was fifty-six years old.

I started teaching in the early '70s and have been doing so ever since. I teach six-year-olds, first grade. I've taught kindergarten and preschool, as well. I teach mathematics, science, and peace.

Judith Vladek, 70, New York City. p. 80.

I still get passionately angry and it's what keeps me working. I am angry about the way American industry is treating workers. I am angry on behalf of older workers. I'm angry when I see the most solid corporations destroying their most valuable asset. In every major company today, there is a concerted effort to force workers over fifty to retirement. We're taking people who've worked thirty years for the same company and declaring them dispensable. Kleenex. You can never replace that kind of loyalty, that kind of know-how. When I deal with fifty-five-year-old men, who are unlikely to find any appropriate work for themselves again, I cry for them. I cry for a company that's stupid enough to send them away. I see this happening in every workplace, and I am angry. And when working women decide to have children, does that make them a subclass of employables?

... Things are worse in law firms today simply because women believe it's better. That's a terrible myth. Women are half the law school class today, but how many make partners? Five, ten percent at a maximum. Why are men willing to use all their work, all their energy, and not invite them as partners? Because there's a white male hierarchy. The men are at the top and feel comfortable. They use code language. They like team players and *[witheringly]* their teams are male.

Jessie de la Cruz, 74, Fresno, California. p. 123.

I married when I was young, and I never thought about how long I was going to live. How long am I going to be on this earth? You just live day by day. You get older and you realize there are many things you can do besides just staying home, besides feeling sorry for yourself. There's always something to do, no matter what age, as long as you can get up and walk and talk. There's always hope. We have a saying: *La esperanza muere al último.* Hope dies last. Hope for whatever you want to do. If you can't do it today, there's always tomorrow or the next year. I'm going to spend Christmas with my doctor son in Sacramento, come back and make some tamales for the rest of the family out here. And then I'll get back in action at the Fresno city council. That's my way of enjoying life—doing something.

"What's Wrong with Your Mother?": Representations of Menopausal Women in Television and Film

ANJA ZIMMERMANN

Menopause is anathema in popular culture. The exhaustive collection at New York's Museum of Television and Radio has only two television sitcoms dealing with menopause over a period of more than twenty years.[1] There are virtually no commercials featuring menopausal women, and in Hollywood older women are often limited to an occasional appearance at the periphery of main narratives.[2] However, even from looking at the few representations that do exist, it's evident that the meaning of menopause is far from fixed. There is no such thing as *the* menopause. The concept of menopause as well as the individual experiences of women differ not only culturally and historically, but are influenced by many other factors that determine women's lives. This is obvious from comparing the two sitcoms found at the Museum of Television and Radio, which can be read as spot checks for the changing discourses on menopause from the 1970s to the 1990s.

While the two programs deal with menopause as an exclusively white subject, the 1990 film *Privilege* by the independent director Yvonne Rainer assumes a different stance. In this film menopause is not a given fact but a notion, the meaning of which is established along intersecting axes of sexist and racist discourses. Although originating in different spheres of cultural production (commercial TV and independent film) all three treatments can be read as examples of the visual and narrative (de)construction of the menopausal woman. A focus on images of the female body in the representations of menopausal women in popular culture reveals underlying notions of that body as deficient, threatening, and "grotesque." Furthermore, the concept and processes of normalcy as a desired state of bodies, families, and relationships comes into question. How is this normalcy represented, constructed, or questioned through the different stories about menopause? By examining Yvonne Rainer's *Privilege*, it's possible to see how menopause can be visualized in ways beyond the popular imaginations of the menopausal body as "other." This film not only displaces existing stereotypes but also employs specific visual strategies to subvert prevailing representations. The strategies used in the film are a valuable model for challenging the ways that menopause has been formulated and presented in popular imagery.

1. One is an episode of *All in the Family* from 1972, entitled "Edith's Problem"; the other is the 1996 episode of *Cybill* entitled "When You're Hot, You're Hot."

2. For a survey of the marginalization of aging women in popular culture see Betty Friedan, *The Fountain of Age* (New York: Simon and Schuster, 1993).

The idea that menopausal women have bodies that don't fit patriarchal norms of ideal femininity is what structures the narrative of an episode of *All in the Family* entitled "Edith's Problem."[3] The title is revealing, because it is Edith's family that has a "problem" with a mother's and wife's sudden misbehavior. Everybody but Edith is working on Edith's problem. Accordingly, a substantial part of the episode shows the efforts of various family members to explain to Edith that she *has* a problem. Edith's body is different from the beginning; in the very first scene she rushes into the living room, screaming and cursing. In contrast to the calm and often static bodies of her daughter, her son-in-law and her husband, hers is excessive, hysterical, and ever-changing. At one moment it is the "good" body which belongs to a "good" mother who serves the family dinner; the next it is the strange and unfamiliar body of a raging woman who begins throwing things. It has become dysfunctional, and the story revolves around the question of how Edith's behavior can be normalized. To express this visually, the body of the woman is stereotyped as excessive and hysterical and therefore a threat to the structure of the family itself. Consequently, the restoration of normalcy is pursued by reintegrating the raging and dysfunctional woman into the given order.

But why is the focus, both visually and in terms of the narrative, almost exclusively on her body? Why is it Edith's *body* that offends by being so different? I think it's not only because menopause is considered a sign of age located in the female body, but also because the body itself speaks, becoming a symbol for the social order. A literally disordered body can therefore be understood as a symbol for a disruption of social arrangements.

The concept of the "grotesque body" as described in the writings of the Russian theorist Mikhail Bakhtin is useful for understanding these non-idealized body images. Bakhtin's work deals with the carnival as a ritualistic spectacle that existed beyond the control of the church or the state during the Middle Ages. Much more than today's carnivals, these precursors opposed official culture and showed the "relativity of prevailing truths and authorities."[4] During these historical carnivals the official aspect of life, with its emphasis on the stability of social roles and the well-behaved body, was annulled. Instead a different body was staged, one that Bakhtin accordingly named the "grotesque body." The grotesque body is fundamental to the carnivalesque precisely because it expresses displacements in the social order. Hence, the grotesque body refers to "the human body as multiple, bulging, over- or under-sized, protuberant, and

3. Critical analyses have addressed this notion of an imperfect or defective female body during menopause. See Sandra Coney, *The Menopause Industry: A Guide to Medicine's "Discovery" of the Midlife Woman* (Melbourne: Spinifex, 1993).

4. Sue Vice, *Introducing Bakhtin* (Manchester: Manchester University Press, 1997), p. 154.

incomplete. The openings and orifices of this carnival body are emphasized, not its closure and finish."[5]

The body described here is the body that belongs to the Other, the body that is deemed inappropriate, the body that needs to be altered to meet the standards of normalcy. Edith's body is indeed multiple and incomplete because of its random changes from the well-functioning body of the mother/wife to the intemperate menopausal body. It is indisputable that Edith's body is a fundamental threat to the smooth functioning of the family, the locus where this threat is staged and made visible. If one agrees that the body and its images do in fact have a social dimension, then it's obvious why there is such a great need to discipline it. It is potentially transgressive and subversive because its grotesqueness puts into question the ideals associated with the classical body and its conformity with social order. It is important to bear in mind, though, that the symptoms (excessiveness, hysteria) and the cause (menopause) cannot simply be attached to a fixed understanding of how menopausal women are. Accordingly, feminists have convincingly argued for a critical review of the complex functioning of the biomedical knowledge which both defines and produces what is then described as menopause (or, for that matter, femininity, normalcy, health, pathology, etc.).[6] "Edith's Problem" is a case in point; it is scientific authority that confirms the state of her body as menopausal and refers to it as problematic. Edith's daughter Gloria sends the male members of the household away so she can talk to her mother woman to woman. However, male scientific authority is quickly reestablished by Gloria's reference to an article written by "an important doctor who knows everything about it." In this article the symptoms of menopause are referred to as "unpleasant manifestations" that will be eliminated by medical authority. In joking about not knowing what is happening to her body, Edith actually outlines a sad story of female estrangement from it: "When I was a young girl I didn't know what every young girl should know. Now I'm an old lady and I don't know what every old lady should know."

The normalcy that was threatened by Edith's condition is made explicit in the very last scene when her husband Archie (expressing a wish more than a fact) says: "Everything is back to normal now." However, before he even gets to finish his sentence, Edith starts screaming again. All attempts to normalize her seem to fail. This becomes apparent when Gloria gives her mother a pair of false eyelashes to make her "look younger" and give her the feeling that she is still desirable. Archie eventually finds this feminine prop floating in his soup at the dinner table. Edith's inability to fulfill expectations is manifest in her body's refusal to keep the eyelashes on.

5. Peter Stallybrass and Allon White, *The Politics and Poetics of Transgresssion* (Ithaca, N.Y.: Cornell University Press, 1986), p. 9.

6. Much of this criticism is informed by the work of Michel Foucault. See Roe Sybylla, "Situating Menopause within Strategies of Power: A Genealogy," in *Reinterpreting Menopause: Cultural and Philosophical Issues,* eds. Paul Komesaroff, Philipa Rothfield, and Jeanne Daly (London: Routledge, 1997). An early and influential work on how the seemingly empirical facts of "health" and "disease" are inseparably connected with political and sociological fields is Georges Canguilhem, *The Normal and the Pathological* (New York: Zone Books, 1991) which was first published in France in 1966.

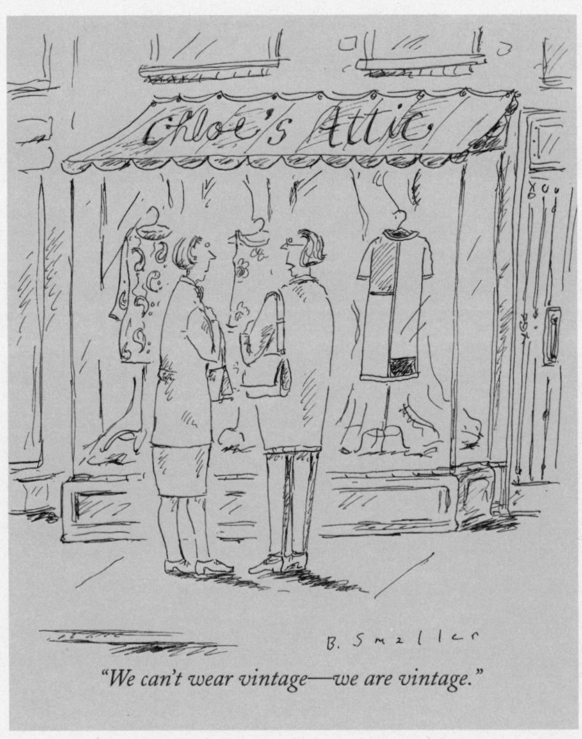

"We can't wear vintage—we are vintage."

Barbara Smaller. ©The New Yorker Collection 1999 Barbara Smaller from cartoonbank.com. All Rights Reserved.

The question, of course, is what is normalcy and by whom is it defined. Significantly, at one point Edith asks her daughter, "What's wrong with your father?" and immediately we hear the recorded laughter that is standard in American sitcoms. The prescribed humor points to the fact that it is indeed a question of viewpoint to determine what's wrong with whom. Although it is assumed to be evident to everybody, including the audience, that Edith is the person who is wrong in the most literal sense, her behavior could be easily read as indicating the contrary. Hence, when Archie returns from a doctor's appointment, he expresses his relief that the doctor prescribed some medication. Again, recorded laughter is heard because Archie takes the pills himself—the medication is not meant for his wife, but to help *him* to calm down and cope with his wife's strange ways. In view of the lack of attention to the "problems" of midlife men in our society, it is not surprising that medication for Archie is considered a joke. This again points to the question of who is defining who has what kind of problems. Whereas menopause is seen as a critical time for middle-aged women, men of the same age are "allowed to simply get on with their lives."[7] Interestingly enough, although Archie has to take pills because of (his wife's) menopause, this doesn't make him appear "sick" or different. It is his wife's problem that is actually treated through him. One might argue that this signals an acceptance of Edith's difference, and further, the acknowledgment of men's entanglement

7. Coney, *The Menopause Industry*, p. 93. Coney emphasizes that "although men in mid-life are just as likely as women to have spreading waistlines, thinning hair, and wrinkles, you don't hear a lot about it. There are no medical journals devoted to aging in men, and men's health problems, such as cardiovascular disease, do not get labeled as a 'men's problem.'"

8. William E. Schmidt, "Birth to 59-Year-Old Briton Raises Ethical Storm," *New York Times* (December 29, 1993): A6.

with menopause. But, once again, Archie's problems only originate in his wife's. His behavior is entirely normal, since it has not changed as he's gotten older. He is the same, whereas Edith is different.

Postmenopausal Bliss

While "Edith's Problem" portrays a problem defined by the strange and unpredictable behavior of the menopausal woman, the episode of *Cybill*, "When You're Hot, You're Hot," at least depicts a woman who knows *what* she is experiencing. Seen in a more glamorous setting than the working-class household of "Edith's Problem," Cybill is a divorced, professional woman who lives with her daughter in a beautiful house. Very early in the episode Cybill declares to her friend Maryann that there is no way that she is "becoming invisible." Instead, she plans on becoming a "brassy, in-your-face menopausal woman." Nevertheless, her behavior in many ways resembles Edith's: she is moody, irritable, and sometimes overreactive. Again, it is her body itself that is funny. Like Edith, Cybill is shown as having lost control over it. In a restaurant scene, Cybill takes off several layers of clothing and drops ice cubes into her décolleté in an effort to control a "hot flash." However, there are two important differences between Edith's "strange body" and Cybill's. While Edith seems to disturb the family routine in a more or less subconscious way mostly beyond her control, Cybill fully realizes that her suddenly erratic body might irritate other people, but enjoys it nonetheless. This *new* body becomes a site of *new* pleasures in the very same restaurant scene when, after using the ice cubes to cool her skin, she stands up moaning with pleasure, and moves in an unmistakably sexy way. Not without reason, Maryann says after watching Cybill: "You're turning me on!"

This alludes to another significant difference between "Edith's Problem" and "When You're Hot . . . "—the representation of sexuality. In both shows sexuality is acknowledged only in passing. Edith's main concern is whether her husband will still find her attractive, whereas Cybill, a divorced woman, is not questioning her attractiveness to men. The implication that women's sexuality declines with age is the subtext of Edith's worries and is also part of the notion that women suffer much more from getting older than men do. This is also evident in the discussions surrounding postmenopausal women who have been able to give birth via new reproductive technologies.[8] Most of them have partners of their own age but it is the woman who is considered unnatural or, even worse, a monster. Being reproductive at an older age has completely different meanings for women and men. A man's reproductive activity in later years may be considered a bit extravagant but it indicates precisely that he is *not* old. Or, to again use Bakhtin's notion, a sixty-year-old pregnant woman is seen as "grotesque" whereas a sixty-year-old man becoming a father is still considered "natural," and a sign of his vigorous masculinity.

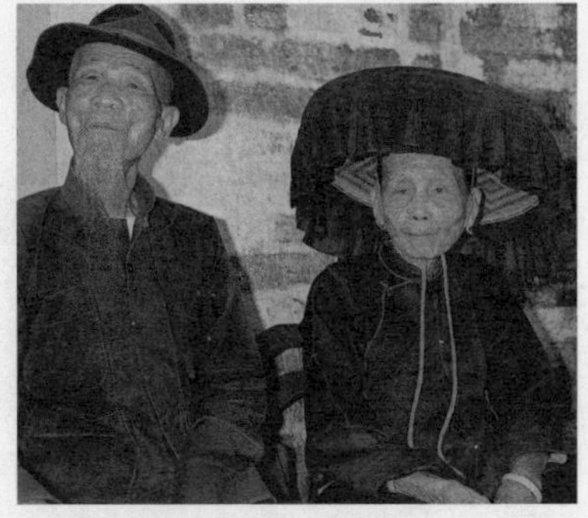

Elder couple from Hong Kong. Published in The Illustrated Encyclopedia of Human Development, *New York: Exeter Books, 1984. ©Robert Harding Associates*

This is why female sexuality during old age, which is defined in women by menopause, is seen as awkward. As female sexuality has always been closely linked to reproductive functions, the presumed end to these abilities makes sexuality itself seem unnatural in the same way that a pregnant sixty-year-old female body is deemed unnatural. Despite an abundance of images of young, white, heterosexual activity in our culture, images that link older women and sexuality seem to be taboo. Partnerships of older men and younger women are considered acceptable, whereas older women and younger men are still the exception, especially if the age difference is more than a few years. When Cybill tells her ex-husband what is happening, he replies: "I'm too young for you to go through menopause," meaning that an "old" (ex-) wife makes him old too, whereas a young one would make *him* young as well.

Getting old not only changes the relationships between (ex-) lovers but also affects virtually every aspect of interaction between the old person and her or his surroundings. The fact that Edith is going through menopause immediately makes her an old person, meaning that she needs help from somebody more competent (i.e., younger). It is significant therefore that Cybill also gets information about menopause from another person, but in this case it's her former mother-in-law, an older woman who smokes pot. She talks about "postmenopausal bliss" and encourages Cybill by telling her that "your life doesn't end just because you go through menopause."

Menopause, "Race,"[9] and Aging in Privilege

"Edith's Problem" and "When You're Hot, You're Hot" both deal with menopause as an isolated problem. As a funny story that fits the demands of television, neither episode presents it as anything more than a problem for a single individual and doesn't take into account how the individual story is profoundly linked to the social and political arenas. In contrast, Yvonne Rainer's *Privilege* is an acute analysis of the stereotypes of aging women, pervasive notions of aging as decline, and the correlation between the marginalization of age and that of "race" in our society. At the same time, *Privilege* questions the division between public and private, or as formulated in early feminist politics, the split between the personal and the political. This formulation is

9. I am well aware that the everyday use of the term "race" in the Anglo-American context is generally not seen as problematic. However, coming from a German background I hesitate to use the word without quotation marks. If one agrees with Robert Miles that "'races' are socially imagined rather than biological realities," then the use of the term is always an expression of racism. Robert Miles, *Racism* (London: Routledge, 1989), p. 71. For a brief introduction that stresses the constructedness of "race" as a (racist) concept, see Ania Loomba, *Colonialism, Postcolonialism* (London: Routledge, 1998), pp. 104–123.

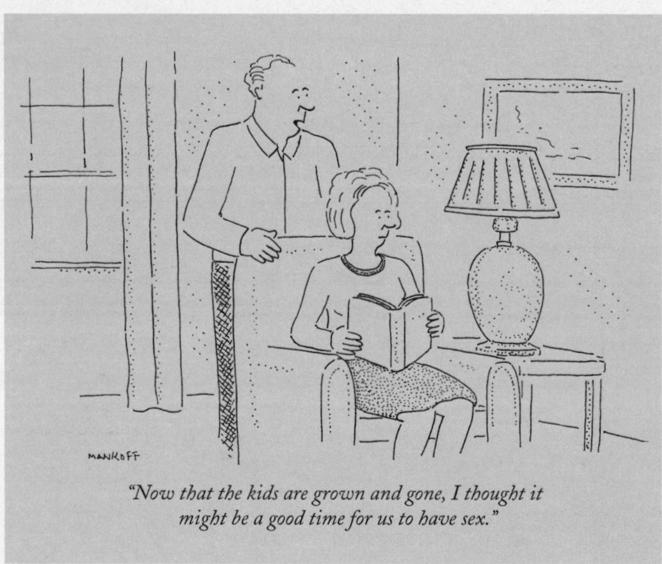

"Now that the kids are grown and gone, I thought it might be a good time for us to have sex."

Robert Mankoff. ©The New Yorker Collection 1999 Robert Mankoff from cartoonbank.com.

a foundation for much of feminist practice and theory, and therefore is particularly applicable to the subject of menopause. Presented by mainstream culture and medical discourse as a personal problem of the aging woman, menopause is linked to paradigms about age, sex, gender, and race. Menopause can be represented as something personal all the more because it is so closely connected to the body. The body as putative site of the natural is used to explain menopause as a fact dictated by changes of the female body. The body therefore has been at the center of recent critical thought, feminist and otherwise, as it has come to be understood as a concept that cannot be separated from culture, constituted as the antonym of nature.[10]

The aesthetic strategies in Rainer's film displace all essentialist notions of menopause. One strategy is the inclusion of black women in the analysis of menopause, providing a cross-cultural discussion. By inserting a film within a film Rainer presents "Yvonne Washington," a black filmmaker working on a documentary on the subject. The textual center of the film is Yvonne Washington's interview with "Jenny,"[11] supplemented by documentary footage from Hollywood movies, interviews conducted by Rainer herself, medical documentaries from the 1960s, and Jenny's "hot-flashbacks." Through Yvonne Washington, Rainer creates an image of a black woman that subverts existing stereotypes of passivity and invisibility. At the same time, the viewer's ability to identify with the film personas is curtailed by mixing different narrative modes, by the dissimilar appearance of bodies and (their) voices, and by conflating past and present.

10. Judith Butler describes this in the following way: "What constitutes the fixity of the body, its contours, its movements, will be fully material, but materiality will be rethought as the effect of power, as power's most productive effect." Judith Butler, *Bodies that Matter: On the Discoursive Limits of Sex* (London: Routledge, 1993), p. 2.

11. Although Jenny's story contains autobiographical allusions to Yvonne Rainer, the character represents other women as well. This is confirmed by Rainer in an interview with Laura Poitras, Susanne Fairfax, and Kurt Easterwood published in Yvonne Rainer, *Talking Pictures: Film, Feminism, Psychoanalysis, Avant-garde* (Bloomington: Indiana University Press, 1989). Also, "Jenny" is played by different actresses.

As a result, seeing *Privilege* is quite different from seeing "Edith's Problem" or "When You're Hot. . . . " In it there is not *one* coherent story that begins, develops, and ends. Instead we hear different voices telling one story or we see a body in one space-time continuum and hear its voice coming from another. The documentary footage from the 70s, for example, is not presented as the neutral bearer of information but as part of the different discourses that are producing "menopause." Because it's difficult to describe all the different threads of the film, I instead want to focus on how it displaces the usual ways of representing menopause.

Jenny's story functions as a recurring narrative, and the interviews with her are interwoven with investigations of racism. A scene intercut in film noir style presents extensive quotations from Frantz Fanon and Eldridge Cleaver focusing on the connection and difference between racism, sexism, and the oppression of lesbians and gays. The critic E. Ann Kaplan noted that this film noir scene should be understood as a "deliberate pun...on the word 'noir,' which links blackness and the evil part of human nature that noir film brings to the surface."[12] I would also suggest that choosing to film a sequence in *black and white* underlines Rainer's choice to make whiteness (and the privileges granted thereby) a subject of discussion.

Race is closely connected to the body, but with very different effects for blacks and whites.[13] White bodies are seen as somehow being above race, whereas black bodies have come to signify it. This idea is introduced to the viewer in the film noir sequence when the discussion of menopause is opened up to include black-on-white rape and relations between black men and white (lesbian) women (represented by Jenny's lesbian friend Brenda). The rapist is personified by three men: Brenda's Hispanic neighbor Carlos, Stuart, who is black, and an unnamed white man. In the beginning we see and hear Stuart and/or the white man quoting a passage from Eldridge Cleaver about raping white women out of revenge. This scene is effectively positioned in another frame of reference by the voiceover of Yvonne Washington, who repeatedly comments on Jenny's flashback by interrupting the narrative: "Jenny, why are you telling me all this? I don't need to hear how Eldridge Cleaver raped women to save the black race. He made a much bigger contribution than inflaming white paranoia." What follows is a pivotal scene in terms of juxtaposing questions of the amalgamation of sexism and racism, or the "dual aversion to blacks and women." Carlos pushes Brenda across the room while she is explaining how femaleness and blackness are constructed in similar ways. Both function as the "other" for the white male, for whom blacks/women are seen as body/matter, while he pictures himself as pure mind.

12. E. Ann Kaplan, "Resisting Pathologies of Age and Race: Menopause and Cosmetic Surgery in the Films by Rainer and Tom," in *Reinterpreting Menopause*, eds. Komesaroff, Rothfield, and Daly, p. 117.

13. See Richard Dyer, *White* (London: Routledge, 1997), p. 30. For the pervasive notion that representations of blacks can be described as dealing with "race" whereas representations of whites are read as individual, but not representative of their "race," see my article, "Identität de/chiffriert: Zu einigen Arbeiten von Zoe Leonard, Cheryl Dunye und Cindy Sherman," *Frauen Kunst Wissenschaft* (August 1997): 12–19.

14. Kaplan, "Resisting Pathologies of Age and Race," p. 118.

15. David Laderman, "Interview with Yvonne Rainer," in *Interventions and Provocations: Conversations on Art, Culture, Resistance*, ed. Glenn Harper (New York: State University of New York Press, 1998), p. 161.

Yvonne Washington immediately challenges this psychoanalytically informed account of racism/sexism by insisting on a historical and economic explanation. In addition, she points out how the alliance of Brenda and Carlos against the "white man" helps to veil Jenny's/Brenda's own entanglement in racism: "White women always manage to use their own victim status as a way of pleading innocent to the charge of racism." We see this further illustrated in a flashback scene: Carlos's girlfriend Digna is accompanying Jenny and her lover on a car trip. Digna, dressed in a Carmen Miranda costume, is not only criticizing "Hollywood's most outrageous Latin American stereotype"[14] but also illustrating the racism of Jenny, who does not notice her while she is sitting in the back of the car talking to the viewer. As a Latin American woman, Digna is bound to be invisible for the white woman, Jenny.

In the interviews Jenny reflects upon the fact that being desired by men was the "linchpin of my identity." *Privilege* explores the ways in which ideas about aging are connected with dominant ideas of female sexuality. In a recent interview Rainer herself describes how she became interested in aging, "which, for a woman, very much has to do with attitudes about sexuality."[15] We have seen that in popular culture this subject is relegated to the margins. However, it is always there as a subtext, more or less able to become manifest in a given narrative. Edith's concern about her attractiveness and Cybill's open enjoyment of her menopausal body (without worries about male approval) should be read as negotiating these very questions: What does it mean for women to live in a society which objects to the idea of postmenopausal women as sexual beings? How are representations of the menopausal body influenced by this idea? And how can subjectivity and desire be reinscribed into our understanding of menopause and aging?

In *Privilege,* sexuality takes center stage. Jenny vigorously speaks out against the "screwed up morality that denies middle-aged women the right to be beautiful, loving, and idealized by men" and tells how she was traumatized by the loss of male admiration. And yet, although she has lost the privilege of being desired by men, she still has the privilege of whiteness, which profoundly shapes her knowledge of reality. The title of Rainer's film therefore refers to the multiple privileges (or lack thereof) conferred by race, age, and/or gender. The many discourses that are invoked—medical, feminist, racial—are shown to partake in the everyday manifestations of privilege or discrimination.

Conclusion: Resisting the Normalizing Narrative

What are we to make of these divergent images of menopausal women? Of Edith and her lost eyelashes swimming in her husband's soup? Of Cybill and her intention to be a "brassy, in-your-face menopausal woman"? Of the manifold, interlined, and complicated stories about aging, racism, and sexism told in Rainer's film?

The notion of the grotesque body, as applied by cultural and feminist critics, may be the key.[16] As I've argued above, Edith's strident menopausal body can be read as grotesque and therefore disruptive to the social order. The menopausal woman embodies transgressive qualities, hence images of menopausal women in popular culture hint at the potentially transgressive quality of menopause itself. It is not only Edith who subverts an important institution of patriarchal control, the traditional family. In a similar way, Cybill's ex-mother-in-law is the antithesis of approved grandmotherly behavior as she speaks openly about "postmenopausal bliss," indicating that after menopause the options for female pleasure and control are increasingly diverse. However, it would be a mistake to interpret these popular images as transgressive simply because they portray menopausal women as shrill, reactive, loud, disturbing, and grotesque, for this would play into and reinforce stereotypes about hysterical women. In addition, the mass-media representations of menopausal women reviewed here juxtapose a grotesque female body with a normal male body. Both images work together. The alleged normalcy of the male body, which also ages but is never staged as such, is strengthened by the excessiveness of the female body. The grotesqueness of the female body serves as a foil to the perfect male body which is presented to us as if oblivious to its own gravity. While changes that occur in later life are mostly stereotyped as negative for both men and women, it is still only the woman for whom those changes are marked by the concept of menopause. Hence, it could be argued that the very grotesqueness of the female body in the end reinstalls the social order.

On the other hand, there is no transgression without a transgressive reader. Yvonne Rainer's film serves as a model for a perspective that takes existing discourses, rearranges them, and appropriates them for new, contradictory purposes.[17] Her approach has to be carefully distinguished from the mechanisms of popular culture insofar as she deliberately works against the sexist and/or racist narratives that inform mass culture representations. *Privilege* literally shows that there is not *one* story about menopause, or even *one* menopause. The different modes of representing it—medical discourse, documentary, fiction—

16. For examples, see Mary Russo, *The Female Grotesque: Risk, Excess, Modernity* (London: Routledge, 1994); Mary Russo, "Female Grotesques: Carnival and Theory," in *Feminist Studies/Critical Studies*, ed. Teresa de Lauretis (Bloomington: Indiana University Press, 1986) and Marcia Tucker, "The Attack of the Giant Ninja Mutant Barbies," in *Bad Girls*, Marcia Tucker, et al. (New York: New Museum of Contemporary Art; Cambridge, Mass.: The MIT Press, 1994).

17. The use of the Carmen Miranda costume and the quotation from educational material from the 1960s are only two examples among many.

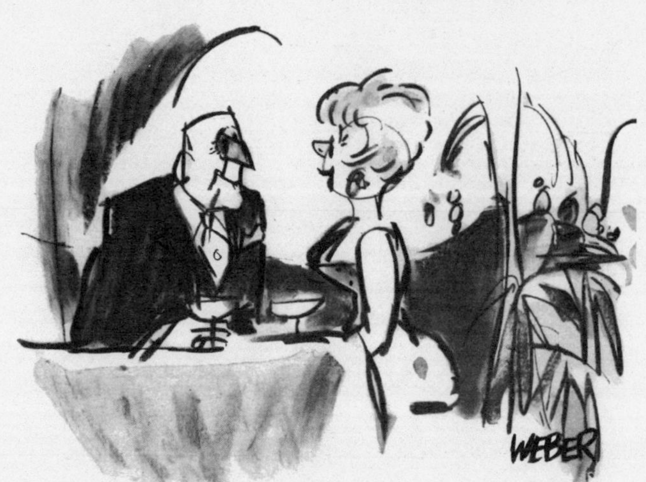

"Gee whizz, Mr. Curtis, a million dollars isn't old!"

are juxtaposed in order to disrupt any single authoritarian voice. Therefore, the transgression actually resides in the *strategies* that are employed to "topple the centrality of the colonialist male voice."[18] Likewise, an understanding of the images of menopausal women as transgressive in popular culture coincides with feminist reflections on the relationship between a text (a film, an artwork, etc.), the critic, and the process of interpretation:

> . . . [A] fully politicized feminist criticism has seldom been content . . . to take the measure of already-constituted subjectivities: it has aimed, rather, at bringing into being new meaning. . . [I]t may be said to have a performative dimension—i.e., to be doing something beyond restating already existent ideas and views.[19]

Privilege is indeed creating new meaning. Menopause is no longer exclusively a story told by white women. Men are added to the picture, in order to enable us to see that it is a male medical establishment that is telling women what menopause means. Unlike "Edith's Problem," in which Edith's daughter refers her mother to an all-knowing male doctor, *Privilege* effectively questions this hierarchy of knowing and not-knowing. The male medical discourse is therefore no longer the authoritative voice. And, by unmasking male discourse, Rainer encourages the viewer to respond differently to these authoritative voices the next time s/he encounters them. But *Privilege* is not an answer; its achievement lies precisely in raising questions. What exactly is the threat

18. David Laderman, "Interview with Yvonne Rainer," in *Interventions and Provocations: Conversations on Art, Culture, Resistance*, ed. Glenn Harper (New York: State University of New York Press, 1998), p. 161.

19. Tania Modleski, "Some Functions of Feminist Criticism, or the Scandal of the Mute Body," *October* 49 (1983): 13–14.

of the grotesque menopausal body to society? How is ageism interlinked with racism? Why is menopause a sign of old age that only women seem to bear? What, historically, has been the role of male doctors in disseminating exclusive knowledge about it? *Privilege* invites us to broaden our view of menopause beyond its meaning as an inevitable sign of female decline. The meaning of male menopause, for example, may not be explicitly discussed in *Privilege*, but it is implicit in the fact that women seem to "age longer and better," as Betty Friedan puts it.[20] Although older men enjoy significant privileges compared to older women, their aging is influenced by the fact that the definition of masculinity is strongly tied to the notion of youth.[21] Consequently, there is a conflict between the familiar representation of male agency, aggression, and domination, and a view of the aging process as antagonistic to these attributes of masculinity. The helplessness, disorientation, and, one could argue, the femaleness associated with age narrow the possibilities for both women and men. However, the connection between age and traditionally female attributes supports the almost exclusive focus on female aging as a problem in our society.

All this is a reason to carry on with reading the existing images of menopause, however stereotyped they may be, as material that waits to be reappropriated, subverted, and unmasked.

20. Friedan, *The Fountain of Age*, p. 133.

21. Ibid., p. 165.

*"I have everything now I had twenty years ago—
except now it's all lower."*

—Gypsy Rose Lee

Stephen Katz, Disciplining Old Age: The Formation of Gerontological Knowledge *(Charlottesville and London: University Press of Virginia, 1996), p. 1.*

Aging and old age are intrinsic to every form of knowledge and cultural practice: spiritual, ritual mythical, symbolic, artistic, metaphorical, and architectural. They are the central organizing resources for a multitude of social structures from nomadic pastoralism to complex kinship systems to statelike bureaucracies. Indeed, aging and old age have been so diversely and richly understood that no single knowledge of them is universal. Nor should it be. The meanings of aging and old age are scattered, plural, contradictory, and enigmatic. They are confirmation that the mysteries of age have furnished the human imagination with limitless opportunities to express itself. Age is everywhere, but the world's cultures have taught us that age has no fixed locus.

***Betty Friedan*, The Fountain of Age** *(New York: Simon and Schuster, 1993), pp. 28, 30–31.*

One day during a discussion of "those poor old senile people" in nursing homes, I suddenly heard myself saying, "Let's not talk about 'them,' let's talk about 'us.'" I had come to understand, through my own experience, the panic that trapped those of us who are growing older into clutching at the illusion of physical youth. . . . Now that I could honestly think about "them" as "us," I came to realize that the fountain of age didn't mean, can't mean, the absence of physiological, emotional, or situational change. But it takes so much effort to hold on to the illusion of youth, to keep the fear of age at bay, that in doing so we could fail to recognize the new qualities and strengths that might emerge.

. . . I have discovered that there is a crucial difference between society's image of old people and "us" as we know and feel ourselves to be. There are truly fearful realities reflected—and imposed—by that image. To break through that image, we must first understand why, how, and by whom it is perpetuated. We must also glimpse some new possibilities and new directions, both as individuals and as a society, that belie that image. I have found the answers to many of the questions that motivated my quest to distinguish the truth from the lies, the realities from the myths, about age. I have also found that there are choices we can make along the journey we all, sooner or later, must take that truly open surprising new possibilities.

***Kathleen Woodward*, Aging and Its Discontents: Freud and Other Fictions** *(Bloomington: Indiana University Press, 1991), p. 193.*

One of the unresolved questions . . . is the extent to which we can alter or inflect our experience of aging and advanced old age by changing our representations of it. Certainly our old age—our various experiences of old age—are inseparable from our culture's representations of aging. Certainly the profound gerontophobia in our culture should be extirpated, and one of the ways to begin that process is to examine critically our representations of aging and to work to produce new ones. . . . [I]n the West the dominant trope of aging has been the decay and decline of the body. . . . [W]e adopt many defenses to deal with our anxiety. We repress the subject of aging. We relegate aging to others. We do not recognize it in ourselves. And as I have insisted, it is only with great effort and perhaps even courage that our culture will rewrite its discourses about aging.

***Margaret Morganroth Gullette, "Midlife Discourses," in* Welcome to Middle Age! (And Other Cultural Fictions), *ed. Richard A. Shweder* ***(Chicago: University of Chicago Press, 1998), p. 27.*

A cult of youth that makes youth perishable and irretrievable, an abhorrence of aging that depreciates the middle years and will not decide when they begin—this is still the bodily surface of decline ideology, the bodily binary of its particular power system. This is the peak-and-slide that the dominant culture teaches us to experience as private. Mainstream culture trains us to believe certain ideas, hold certain values, own certain images, practice visual discriminations, feel certain emotions. The audience for it maintains and circulates the age knowledge provided by the ideology, repeating as true its claim to be natural and universal, its perverse undecidability at the one crucial point (when decline begins), its reliance on biology, its stoic harshness.

***Elizabeth Haiken*, Venus Envy: The History of Cosmetic Surgery** *(Baltimore: The Johns Hopkins University Press, 1997), pp. 1–4.*

At the turn of the century, cosmetic surgery appeared to contradict both the traditional American injunction against vanity and the Hippocratic injunction against doing harm. Those surgeons who considered themselves "reputable" (and, as such, undertook to organize the emergent specialty of plastic surgery) believed that by placing healthy patients at risk, cosmetic surgery contradicted the fundamental tenets of the medical profession; "beauty surgery" was the province of quacks and charlatans. Like their physicians, most Americans condemned cosmetic surgery. Big noses, small breasts, and wrinkles of all sizes, they believed, were simply facts of life, and the dignity with which one bore them testified to the strength of one's character.

Americans might have been more comfortable with the idea of cosmetic surgery had they viewed it simply as a newfangled form of the vaunted American tendency toward self-improvement, but they did not. Perfectibility, as originally conceived, was defined in religious (or at least spiritual) terms. The physical culture movement of the late nineteenth and early twentieth centuries did encourage Americans to pursue physical perfection, but its adherents, too, framed this project in terms that, if not specifically religious, were at least imbued with spiritual and moral meaning. Steeped in this tradition, most turn-of-the-century Americans regarded cosmetic surgery with the same suspicion modern fitness enthusiasts display toward new pharmaceutical products like fenfluramine-phentermine (fen/phen) and Redux.

Over the course of this century, these conflicts ceased to pose significant barriers to the profession's growth. *Plastic surgery* (the term encompasses both reconstructive and cosmetic surgery) is now one of the largest and fastest-growing medical specialties in the United States. Its clientele increases yearly in both size and diversity, and the entire body—male as well as female—is now within its purview. According to the American Society of Plastic and Reconstructive Surgeons, Inc., between 1982 and 1992 the number of people who approve of plastic surgery increased by 50 percent, while the number who disapprove decreased by 66 percent.

Cosmetic (or aesthetic) surgery, broadly defined as surgery undertaken solely for reasons of appearance, accounts for an increasing proportion of its growth. Aging faces, flat breasts, and small penises, which as facts of life were considered undeserving of medical attention, have been progressively redefined as problems worthy of medical concern and more recently as pathologies or deformities requiring medical solutions.

***Patricia Mellencamp*, High Anxiety: Catastrophe, Scandal, Age, and Comedy** *(Bloomington: Indiana University Press, 1992), pp. 284–85, 287.*

Age can be both obsession and contradiction, a secret, like sex, which gossip refuses to let us keep—not to tell is a sign of vanity, false pride, dishonesty. The downfall of Gary Hart began, and perhaps ended, when he lied about his age, setting off a calamity of further secrets. After a "certain age," women who proudly tell elicit amazed disavowal: But you don't look fifty! We can be older, but we must not be as old as we are. Women measure themselves and each other across a chasm, a ten-year or greater discontinuity between the real and appearance, a gap literalized by reruns. When I first began to study Lucy [Lucille Ball], I was impressed that she was thirty-eight when preparations began and forty in the first season of broadcast; a forty-year-old female star was unusual by U.S. standards, particularly a star constantly upstaging her husband, desirous of a job, a railing against house-wifery by performing in a man's world of physical comedy.

... [C]onscious conventions of chronological difference reiterate unconscious Freudian desires and taboos: Men's desire for their mothers and women's desires to possess their sons are unconscious prohibitions restaged in the spectacle of the older woman with the younger men—a sensational topic on Phil and Oprah. This rare scenario is not readily accepted, as is the operative and sanctioned reverse—the older man and the younger woman. For, within the Freudian scenario, it is proper that the girl pass on to her father, often elided with husband. Thus, men traverse or can cross the generational divide, while women are rigidly held to their prescribed, chronological role and place. Men are generationally mobile, even without mask or disguise, and thus appear to be younger. Women are fixed within a dated schema of generation. (Cher, realizing overtly that power more than sex is involved in this restriction and more respectably than, for example, Joan Collins, exists as a challenge to the decorum of chronology—although her "looks" belie her age as her costume denies "mother" and thus sanction her actions—living with a twenty-three-year-old man, then a thirty-year-old rocker.)

Signs of Age: Representing the Older Body

PHILIP KOPLIN

"Nothing is ever seen naked or nakedly."

—Nelson Goodman[1]

As you read these words, you're growing older, a fate that befell you the moment you entered the world. That we can know of our bondage to time is one of the more dubious benefits of human self-awareness. Through its effect on our bodies, time enters our evolving sense of who we are and how we and the world interrelate. As we move through life, our bodies eventually take on a particular set of characteristics: skin wrinkles; curves slacken and wander; flesh sags. In general, we don't take such signs merely as indices of *change*. We, and those who see us, read them as symptoms of a process called *aging*, a judgment passed not only on the body, but also on the self it harbors; we see not just an aging body, but an aging *person*, one approaching, or perhaps already belonging to, the social category called "elderly."[2]

The process of seeing things in terms of categories, as meaningful units belonging to meaningful wholes, is a basic necessity of getting about in the world. When applied to people, the process leads to social stereotyping. We experience ourselves and others as members of groupings based on gender, age, ethnicity, etc., and our judgments about people are based largely on what we've learned and been prompted to think about the groups to which we see them assigned (although our judgments may change as we get to know people as individuals, or as we encounter challenges that groups may offer to what they consider to be unjust representations).[3] While stereotyping, or to put it more benignly, classifying, may seem to be an inevitable feature of human perception, the beneficial effects of trust, solidarity, and altruistic behavior that can come from identifying with a given group often have their darker counterparts when we deal with "outsiders": Membership in a group can offer the sanction to deny to others the full humanity we claim for ourselves, and this can result in the rationalization of their mistreatment.

Consider the easy enough identification that someone with a wrinkled face is an "older person." What we initially expect of such a person will depend on our experience of similar people, mediated through what our culture teaches us about them—that they have, say, a decreased capacity to care for themselves

1. *Languages of Art*, 2nd ed. (Indianapolis: Hackett, 1976), p. 8.

2. The phrase "the body" refers in fact to an abstraction: every human body is different, is tied up with the personhood of a particular self, with its own ways of being in the world (see Rosi Braidotti, *Nomadic Subjects. Embodiment and Sexual Difference in Contemporary Feminist Theory* [New York: Columbia University Press, 1994] and Moira Gatens, *Imaginary Bodies. Ethics, Power and Corporeality* [London: Routledge, 1996]). At the same time, these unique bodies and the way we think about them may show "familial" resemblances based on shared biological and cultural history. On the persistence of cultural continuities see, for example, Caroline Walker Bynum, *The Resurrection of the Body in Western Christianity, 200–1326* (New York: Columbia University Press, 1995) on medieval debates on the nature of the "resurrection body":

> ... the doctrine of resurrection has been of enormous consequence in shaping assumptions we still hold concerning personhood and survival. Much of our current Western notion of the individual has taproots in medieval discussions of the ontological significance of the body. If we see the individual as unique—valued yet opaque and unknowable because (in the currently fashionable term) "other"—our assumption is informed by hundreds of years of puzzlement over embodiment. (p. 341)

In fact, for many people the "body" may not be a neat, theoretically coherent concept: they might seek acupuncture for a migraine, take antihistamines for a cold, and use and follow what's going on in the world. It will seem reasonable to take that initial sign of group membership as a marker of those other characteristics as well; thus, we will see a person with a wrinkled face not just as someone who has been alive for a certain number of years, but as someone prone to display at least some of the (generally negative) characteristics we associate with advanced age, and we will treat that person accordingly, not always to their benefit.

A person's age—actual or apparent—is indeed one of the features by which he or she is characterized. Most of us know the dizzying feeling that comes with the attempt to correlate our chronological age with how old we feel and with how old we think our body looks; moreover, others may see us differently than we see ourselves, based on our actions and on the signs that mark our bodies. By how they treat us, people signal what they see us as, just as we do to them. This mutual activity is a significant means by which our selves are formed and maintained. As in any negotiation, the outcome will depend on the relative positions of the parties involved. For example, since the elderly are often at a socioeconomic disadvantage, this makes it easier to reduce them to even further social irrelevance by constructing them as helpless and without agency. They may resist such categorization, through behavior that caregivers and others who encounter them may characterize as "inappropriate"—so that "inappropriate behavior," which may in fact represent attempts by the elderly to assert their autonomy, becomes one more aspect of the category in terms of which they're quite literally kept in their place, as in the sometimes inhumane treatment of recalcitrant elderly in "retirement" homes.

One culturally important way of constructing and imposing identities on people and groups is through the use of visual images. When something is being represented in the form of an image, the person for whom such an image is intended has to know that a message is being sent, and which interpretive codes to apply. The more "natural" these codes seem, the more the viewer will feel that the world being represented is the world as it "really" is. Such messages can have several layers of meaning. For example, when someone, whether through art, advertising, or the news or entertainment media, represents to us a body that they intend us to see as "old," they may be prompting us to make additional inferences about the person involved, or about ourselves, if we're supposed to be seeing ourselves as persons of this type. Consider how advertising tries to convince us that we can control our fate through the right expenditures; in reinforcing the notion that we're only as old as we feel or look, it represents the aging body as prone to a set of infirmities and indignities that appropriate products and treatments can help to disguise or alleviate.

a cure based on "folk" notions of occult sympathy (as formalized for example in Renaissance doctrines of astrological medicine) to treat insomnia, unaware of or indifferent to the possible incompatibility of the body concepts involved. In addition, cultures will vary on how they conceive the relation of body types to social ideals and structures. Thus, one has to consider the existential uniqueness of bodies, their biological commonalities, and the ways in which these factors are constructed and imbued with meaning in differing social and cultural contexts. (Although one needs to guard against what Elizabeth Grosz, in *Space, Time, and Perversion: Essays on the Politics of Bodies* [London: Routledge, 1995], p. 31, calls the discursivization of bodies, and Maxine Sheets-Johnstone, in *The Roots of Power. Animate Form and Gendered Bodies* [Chicago: Open Court, 1994], p. 69, "grammatological creationism.")

3. See Diana Tietjens Meyers, *Subjection and Subjectivity: Psychoanalytic Feminism and Moral Philosophy* (London: Routledge, 1994), for the ways in which subordinated groups may employ "counterfigurations" and "dissident speech" to combat negative stereotypes, foster group self-esteem, and enhance political efficacy, as well as possibly arouse more sympathetic treatment from members of culturally dominant groups. Also see Michel de Certeau, *The Practice of Everyday Life* (Berkeley: University of California Press, 1984), p. 18, on the "innumerable ways of playing and foiling the other's game" available to those who, lacking their own space, "have to get along in a network of already established forces and representations."

"Do not resist growing old—
many are denied the privilege."

—Anonymous

The unfortunate social implications of bearing the signs and symptoms of age have been instilled in us so well by our culture that these unhappy implications—loss of status and social relevance, for example—usually don't need to be spelled out any further. A person not taking the measures being offered against these signs and symptoms presumably is resigned/consigned to whatever calamities the advertising is trying to convince us we can avoid, in this case the misery of being and looking old. The paradox lies in the fact that, if you're only as old as you feel, feeling the need to take measures against feeling old will help reinforce the feeling of feeling old—which will further fuel the advertising/consuming process. Of course, advertisers are also discovering the lucrative over-fifty market, which they hope to reach with more "positive" images of aging. Yet even images of people in their "golden years" warn of the calamities that lurk if one doesn't buy the right products, calamities whose threat increases as one moves deeper into old age.

Advertising aimed at the old or the not-wanting-to-feel-old shows bodies intended to be seen primarily by those targeted groups. In the entertainment media, the audience is broader and the bearers of older bodies are treated with a different range of attitudes. Film and television tend to treat the human body as an ambivalent source of both pleasure and potential disaster. The latter aspect usually comes to the fore with regard to the older body, which is represented as the source of often comic, occasionally poignant frailty. It leaks, it stumbles, its sight and hearing fail along with its memory, its claims to passion are pained and embarrassed if they exist at all. While at least advertising sometimes represents the older body as still capable of certain kinds of pleasure—for instance, after taking vitamin supplements or anti-arthritic medicines, one might go for a walk on the beach with one's gray-haired companion, or play a round of golf, or tend one's rose garden—the capacity of the older body for pleasure is rarely portrayed in film or television, except as a source for scandal or condescending amusement to younger viewers.

The making and presenting of "art" are particular types of culture-specific gestures, the reception of which involves more than the simple translation of intended meanings by an otherwise passive receiver. These responses and

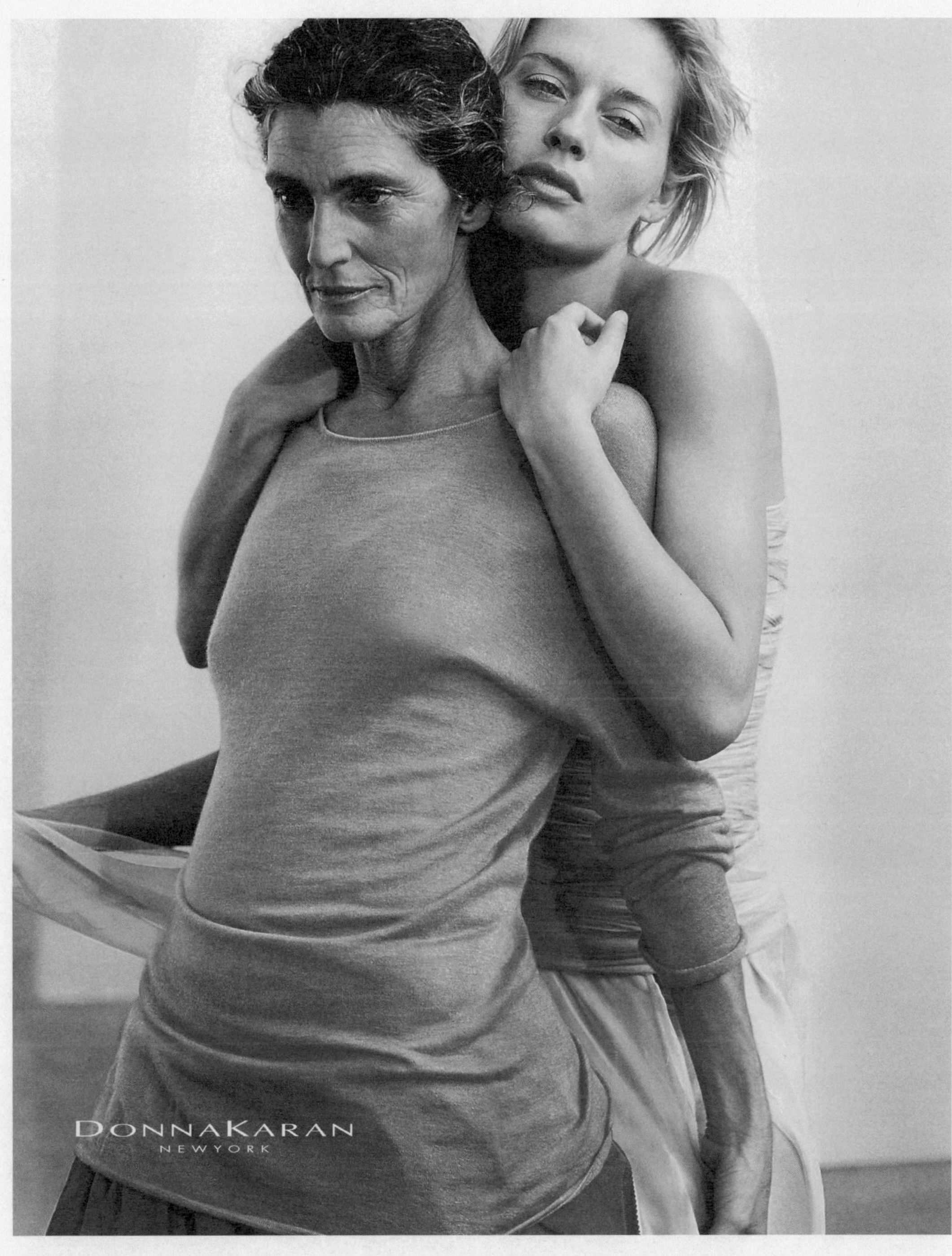

Donna Karan advertisement, *Spring 1999. Bendetta Barcini and Annie Morton, models. Peter Lindbergh, photographer. Courtesy of The Donna Karan Company, New York.*

meanings will result from the interplay of various personal and cultural factors. For example, it would seem that more female than male contemporary artists are examining how images of the body impose and carry social meaning. Women are constantly being made aware of the importance placed on how their bodies look, and dealing with their bodily self-image is a challenge throughout their life course. This self-examination is encouraged and socially sanctioned by the advertising and entertainment media, as well as by feminist challenges to the messages these carry.

While their physical image is an issue for men as well, in general they seem less willing or able to examine its role in establishing their identities, and particularly in carrying out this interrogation communally or in public, perhaps because so large a cultural investment goes into having them *not* question their supposedly natural or God-given socially dominant position. So much of this "natural" superiority is connected to physical prowess and virility that examining or contemplating the decline of his potencies would bring into doubt the basis for a man's "right" to be dominant. This doubt is not something one would expect to see socially encouraged, although the proliferation of "men's groups," both fundamentalist and New Age, along with the increasing media-driven acceptability of "anti-aging" cosmetic practices for men, suggest that masculine roles and identities are indeed being placed in question by various social forces.

What this will mean for the role of aging men remains to be seen, though it seems unlikely that these activities will in themselves lead to any significant challenge to the patriarchal scheme that underlies our social structure. In any event, a man often maintains or even, up to a point, enhances his social position as he gets older, and so, as he ages, his social role is not thrown into question to the same degree as that of an aging woman, whose childbearing capacity fades along (supposedly) with her sexual attractiveness, leaving her to ponder what her role is expected to be and how it came to be tied so strongly to her body.[4]

One of the issues raised by art practices concerns the role of aesthetic judgment in determining how we respond to objects, including people and images of people. While it may be difficult to separate cultural from genetic factors in determining which geometric proportions or human features we find "naturally" pleasing, it seems that we do tend to see people who are physically attractive as also possessing superior inner qualities. This linking of the Beautiful with the Good, which has a long philosophical pedigree, has an unfortunate corollary:

4. Men in our culture are willing to appreciate other male bodies as part of a display of athletic or sexual prowess, but only within social contexts that are carefully constructed to avoid the implications of internalized homophobia—certainly a man dare not be caught looking too fixedly at another man's naked body (a situation perhaps even more fraught with alarming personal implications for someone who catches himself looking), or allow his own body to be subject to the gaze of other men; women seem far less prone to this same-gender fear. It is true that an earlier generation of male performance and "body" artists exposed their naked bodies, but this was usually in the context of pseudoritualistic fantasies of neo-archaic violence and mutilation, in the guise of evoking a more "authentic" experience. Such work tended to direct attention away from the particular body and its fate, toward general, supposedly archetypal meanings, at the same time deflecting potential homosexual "misunderstandings." As this sort of activity has faded from the art scene, this arena has largely been left to more personal, individuated explorations by female artists (although "goddess" manifestations remain a prominent subgenre) as well as by gay male artists, who have been exploring difficult issues related to the body and mortality.

People whose bodies are perceived as being unattractive or undesirable—such as the elderly—will often be seen as lacking full or valuable inner lives, and as representing at the least an affront to tact and good taste, the glue that holds a "civil" society together, and at the worst as being morally defective and not worthy of respect. Moreover, for much of Western history it is not just any "beautiful" body that has signified virtue and right, but a particular variety of body, the body of that paradigmatic specimen of humanity, Christian European Man in the full flower of his intellectual and physical capacities; thus the bodies of Woman, Jew, Black, Cripple, etc., have been constructed and stigmatized in terms of their deviations from that supposed norm; again, seeing a body as being deviant helps justify special, generally pernicious, treatment of the person embodied with it. Persons bearing older bodies are among the victims of this process.

In sum, the advertising and entertainment media emphasize that the way we look determines how we're seen, which sounds innocent enough, until one realizes what they're really saying: that looking a certain way means being a specific type of person, one to be thought of and treated in a specific sort of way; that, for example, people with older bodies, bodies differing from the taut, unmarked ideal body we're encouraged to admire and aspire to, should feel and be treated like "old people," with the generally negative connotations that come with that category. Clearly, art can't depict "the" older body, any more than it can show a body, old or otherwise, prior to cultural inscription. The body is never naked; stripped of its cultural clothing, a body is no/body at all. What art can do is show us how we tend to connect the way someone looks with her or his social value, as well as alert us to the range of persons and attitudes the variety of older bodies, like the variety of bodies in general, can represent.

This essay was initially prepared in connection with the exhibition, Signs of Age: Representing the Older Body, *presented at the Santa Barbara Contemporary Arts Forum, November 8, 1997–January 18, 1998, which I co-organized with Nancy Doll and Anette Kubitza; I thank them as well as Elizabeth A. Brown, Noel Fleming, and Marcia Tucker for their help and suggestions.*

Henry Miller, On Turning Eighty *(Santa Barbara: Capra Press, 1972), pp. 9–11.*

At eighty I believe I am a far more cheerful person than I was at twenty or thirty. I most definitely would not want to be a teen-ager again. Youth may be glorious, but it is also painful to endure. Moreover, what is called youth is not youth, in my opinion; it is rather something like premature old age.

I was cursed or blessed with a prolonged adolescence; I arrived at some seeming maturity when I was past thirty. It was only in my forties that I really began to feel young. By then I was ready for it. (Picasso once said: "*One starts to get young at the age of sixty, and then it's too late.*") By this time I had lost many illusions, but fortunately not my enthusiasm, nor the joy of living, nor my unquenchable curiosity. Perhaps it was this curiosity—about anything and everything—that made me the writer I am. It has never left me. Even the worst bore can elicit my interest, if I am in the mood to listen.

With this attribute goes another which I prize above everything else, and that is the sense of wonder. No matter how restricted my world may become I cannot imagine it leaving me void of wonder. In a sense I suppose it might be called my religion. I do not ask how it came about, this creation in which we swim, but only to enjoy and appreciate it. Much as I may rail about the condition of life in which we find ourselves I have ceased to believe that I can remedy it. I may be able to alter my own situation somewhat but not that of others. Nor do I see that anyone past or present, however great, has been able to truly alter "*la condition humaine.*"

What most people fear when they think of old age is the inability to make new friends. If one ever had the faculty of making friends one never loses it however old one grows. Next to love, friendship, in my opinion, is the most valuable thing life has to offer.

***Kyriakos S. Markides and Manuel R. Miranda,* Minorities, Aging, and Health** *(Thousand Oaks, Cal.: Sage Publications, 1997), pp. 1–3.*

As we approach the end of the 20th century, African Americans continue to be the largest ethnic minority population in the United States, and their numbers are projected to increase by 150% over the next 40 years. Projected increases during the same period are considerably larger for the elderly in other major ethnic minority populations: over 200% among Native Americans, almost 500% among Hispanics, and by well over 500% among Asians/Pacific Islanders. The impact of this growth in numbers of minority elderly is expected to be especially strong in the South and Southwest (U.S. Bureau of the Census, 1992). Hispanic elderly are expected to outnumber African American elderly by the year 2050, and Asian/Pacific Islanders elderly will constitute approximately 7% of the older population by the year 2050, up from 2% in 1995 . . . The Native American population is still relatively young, with only 5% being 65 years or older. Their numbers and proportions of the elderly should increase rapidly in the next several decades . . . Researchers as well as policymakers often ignore the diversity within these minority populations, especially among Hispanics and Asians/Pacific Islanders.

***Jimmy Carter,* The Virtues of Aging** *(New York: The Library of Contemporary Thought, 1998), pp. 88–89.*

We tend to feel that our work defines who we are. In our later years, if we are asked, "Tell me about yourself," we might respond, "I'm retired," and perhaps go on to explain what we used to be. At different times in my life I have introduced myself as a submariner, farmer, warehouseman, state senator, governor, or even president, if that was necessary. I might have added where I lived, but that was about it. Now, even though not holding a steady job, I could reply, depending on my audience, that I am a professor, author, fly fisherman, or woodworker. I could add American, southerner, Christian, married, or grandfather. The point is that each of us is a complex human being, with multiple choices of our primary interests or identification at any moment. Keeping a number of these options alive is a good indication of the vitality of our existence.

Marjorie M. Schweitzer, "The Elders: Cultural Dimensions of Aging in Two American Indian Communities," in Growing Old in Different Societies, *ed. Jay Sokolovsky (Acton, Mass.: Copley Publishing Group, 1987), pp. 170–171.*

Evidence shows that in spite of the lack of economic or political power today, some [American] Indian aged are able to occupy positions of power and prestige because of the cultural contributions they can make. This is especially true when the revival of moribund ceremonies and rituals depends directly on the knowledge that the elders have . . . The younger generation, on the other hand, identifies with the individual rather than the group, future orientation, mastery over nature, and on doing rather than being. The younger generation readily acknowledges whites as their reference group.

Robert L. Kahn, Ph.D. and John W. Rowe, M.D., Successful Aging *(New York: Random House Publishers, 1998), pp. 5, 80.*

There have been two major phases in the improvement of life expectancy during the past two centuries. The first was a reduction in infant mortality and death rates in childhood in the nineteenth and early twentieth centuries; the second, a more recent decrease in death rates among middle-aged and older people. Improvements in life expectancy for children are largely due to better prenatal and perinatal care, availability of clean water, increases in food supply, and control of infectious diseases such as smallpox, yellow fever, tuberculosis, and fatal forms of pneumonia. Ninety-eight out of 100 babies born today in the most prosperous nations will live into adulthood. Accidents and, especially in the United States, homicides are now greater dangers to young people than infectious diseases. A direct effect of reduction in childhood death rates is an increase in the proportion of the population that survives to later ages. In the year 1900, only 19 percent of the individuals who died were over age sixty-five. Today, 72 percent of the deaths occur in that age group. Fifty-eight percent of women born in 1900 survived to age sixty-five, and 25 percent survived to age eighty-five. Of women born in the year 1990, almost 90 percent are expected to live to age sixty-five, and more than half will live to age eighty-five.

. . . Just as no two people are alike, so their physiological health—that is, the functional capacity of their major body organs—varies dramatically. This variability between individuals tends to increase substantially with advancing age. Thus it is fair to say that the older people become, the more dissimilar they become. If you have seen one old person, you have not seen them all. We must fight the tendency to overgeneralize about the health and abilities of older people.

Vern L. Bengston and Leslie A. Morgan, "Ethnicity and Aging: A Comparison of Three Ethnic Groups," in Growing Old in Different Societies, *ed. Jay Sokolovsky (Acton, Mass.: Copley Publishing Group, 1987), p. 158.*

Like other older people in industrial societies, ethnic aged experience the devaluation of old age found in most modern societies. Unlike other older people, however, these aged must bear the additional economic, social, and psychological burdens of living in a society in which racial equality remains more myth than fact.

Old Dogs, New Tricks

ANNE ELLEGOOD

We've all heard the clichés "you can't teach an old dog new tricks," "over the hill," "old maid," "dirty old man,"and numerous others. Familiar images and impressions of the "elderly" spring to mind—frail, wrinkled, stubborn, needy, demanding, old-fashioned, miserly, prudish. When confronted with a non-derogatory image of an older person, we're apt to realize how rare it is to see depictions of elders in general, and even more so those that deliberately challenge the idea that aging is an unfortunate disease to be avoided.

This visual absence and bias extends into the canon of Western art history where representations of elders, particularly as the *subject* of an artwork, are rare. In contemporary art, artists such as John Coplans, Lucien Freud, and Alice Neel have chosen the middle-aged and elder figure as their subject, although these portrayals are not necessarily emblematic of a concern with the aging process itself. The lack of images of the aged in art may find its roots in past centuries, when forty was considered old. Depictions of aging have changed dramatically over time and reflect the predominant beliefs of each period, but nonetheless childhood, adolescence, and young adulthood have remained the favored stages of life in visual culture. In his book *Centuries of Childhood: A Social History of Family Life*, Philippe Ariès claims that every period of history privileged a particular stage of the human life. He argues that "youth" was the preferred age in the seventeenth century and childhood in the nineteenth. As is easily assessed through our daily experiences of media coverage, product marketing, fashion, and popular culture, adolescence and young adulthood are the favored ages of the late twentieth century.

The emphasis on youth did not always exist, however. Medieval art until the twelfth century rarely included images of childhood. This was not because of the artists' inability to portray children, but was rather a reflection of the socio-cultural climate. The Medieval period did not place a great value on children; dependency in childhood was short-lived, and adulthood was the stage of life that was considered to represent the majority of the populace. When images of children did grace artworks of the time, there was little attempt to depict them as they actually looked. Rather, children were simply portrayed as very small adults—the scale of the human figure was reduced, and the physical details that differentiate children from adults were essentially ignored. One can find numerous images of the Christ child in paintings up until the fourteenth century in which he looks like a very small adult male.[1] In the context of this historical framework, it becomes apparent that the lack of representations of the elderly in recent years similarly reflects the social order—one that clearly delineates the stages of life and places greater value, and subsequently greater attention, on particular times of life.

1. See Ariès, Philippe. *Centuries of Childhood: A Social History of Family Life* (New York: Vintage Books, 1965), pp. 32–33.

However, more complex images of elders that attempt to break down the conventional narrow representations we are so used to seeing are on the rise. As the average life expectancy continues to increase and the public's interest in the issues surrounding aging grows, visual images of the aging process and of elders likewise increase. Using a remarkable variety of media and artistic strategies, the works in *The Time of Our Lives* examine such pertinent topics as the invisibility of the aging body, sexuality among the elderly, important stages in the life cycle, medical technology's impact upon reproduction and longevity, attempts to mask the physical signs of aging, fear of dying, the passage of time and the methods and markers employed to track it, the differences in attitudes toward the elderly across cultures, and intergenerational relationships. From figurative painting to a minimalist cube to performance documentary to conceptual installation, the work in the exhibition offers multiple interpretations and representations of age and aging.

Jacqueline Hayden's photographs address the tendency to present youthful beauty at the expense of images of the middle-aged and older, particularly in that venerable tradition in Western painting, the nude. Elderly subjects may be portrayed as the attendants to youthful nudes, but are rarely seen disrobed themselves. In response, Hayden has created a series of silver gelatin photographic prints titled *Figure Model*. Hayden places middle-aged and older models in the familiar poses of the figures of well-known old master works, altering them when appropriate to underscore her reformulation of these historical images. In the piece seen here, Hayden refers to the Mannerist painter Bronzino's allegorical painting *Venus, Cupid, Folly, and Time,* circa 1546. In the Bronzino, the nude, young, and beautiful Cupid is depicted embracing his equally nude, young, and beautiful mother Venus, cupping her breast and allowing her nipple to protrude from between his fingers. The canvas is filled with several other figures, including personifications of Folly and Time, and a number of objects symbolizing concerns of the day. Cupid and Venus are seen in the foreground against a backdrop of busy imagery embodying many painterly preoccupations of the time. The overall impression is of a cramped, ambiguous space with twisted and distorted figures and no particular context or focal point.

"Old age takes away from us what we have inherited and gives us what we have earned."

—Gerald Brenan

In Hayden's version, the context of the action is also ambiguous because the artist has eliminated all imagery in the background, thereby emphasizing the figures themselves, which are nude, seated, and facing front. Bronzino's characters are completely self-absorbed, whereas Hayden's Cupid is an older man who stares out at the viewer while he awkwardly pinches the nipple of a middle-aged Venus between his thumb and index finger. Hayden's Venus gazes to the side, her expression completely affectless. She rests one hand on Cupid's knee, while the other hand is delicately posed in mid-air in front of her body in a configuration not unlike that in the Bronzino. Hayden's figures are unabashed and at ease in their nudity, in defiance of Western culture's distaste for the wrinkles and added girth of the aging body. The artist's use of large format prints makes the figures nearly life-sized, forcing the viewer to confront images of "elderly" nude bodies as perfectly natural, graceful, and elegant rather than as something hidden, deemed unworthy of consideration, and therefore banished as the subject matter of art.

There are few examples of self-portraiture by artists as they enter their later years, the best known of which is perhaps Rembrandt's profoundly honest and realistic depiction of himself in his old age. Among the various examples of contemporary self-portraiture in *The Time of Our Lives* is Harriet Casdin-Silver's three-paneled life-sized holographic work *70 + 1*. In the portrait, Casdin-Silver is nude. She stands balancing on one foot, the other resting on the interior calf muscle of her standing leg. She lovingly cups her breasts in her hands and tilts her head to one side, her eyes closed as if in deep contemplation. Her beauty and the calm that seems to envelop her are striking. *70 + 1* is a subjective examination of the artist's aging body as well as an offering of herself to viewers, both as a physical vessel which has undergone the aging process and as a unique individual with a conscience, a personal history, and an emotional makeup. The artist's use of the hologram, which creates the illusion of three-dimensionality on a two-dimensional surface, allows Casdin-Silver to visually traverse the gap between materiality and ephemerality, body and mind, reality and the fantastic, and to actively engage viewers by requiring that they move through time and space to view the work.

In Yoshiko Kanai's self-portrait drawing *In a Mirror*, the artist represents herself in the act of creating her own image. She is nude and seated in a child-sized chair in a room cluttered with her artistic tools. A pad of paper rests on her lap and she holds a pencil in one hand. She sits in front of a tall mirror and gazes directly at the viewer. Kanai has created an unsettling environment with several disjunctive points of view; reflections appear in surprising places, multiple planes divide the space, and the exact placement of the mirror(s) is elusive. In her work, Kanai explores her role in a society in which women are expected to put the needs of others ahead of their own. Japanese women are taught to present a demeanor of calmness and contentment; to express emotions openly in public is considered inappropriate. Here, Kanai's face has the disembodied look of a mask; her expression is controlled, and she is represented as the idealized middle-aged Japanese woman—quiet, calm, beautiful, neutral. At the same time, she holds one hand up to her chin as if at any moment she may remove the mask and reveal the truth beneath. Seated in a child's chair, she looks awkwardly large, in notable contrast to the diminutive, doll-like quality found in most representations of Japanese women. In Japan, public nudity is taboo; although young women are experiencing some loosening of social mores, middle-aged women are made to feel ashamed if they display any degree of sexuality. With courageous honesty, Kanai draws the curves of her figure, the landscape of her skin, and the true proportions of her body, rejecting an idealization of the body while simultaneously portraying herself as a sexual being.

The Japanese photographer Manabu Yamanaka confronts the same taboo, but unlike Kanai, he is the viewer, and the older Japanese women (who look to be in their eighties) he photographs are the objects being viewed. In *Gyahtei*, his series of black and white prints, the women are nude, shown frontally, standing in a blank white space and gazing directly into the camera. The photographs are apt to make us aware of how infrequently visual culture offers such realistic portrayals. Young viewers in particular may realize that they know very little about the bodily manifestations of aging. Because of this, the images can appear shocking, but the trust in the eyes of Yamanaka's subjects and the vulnerability of their exposure also give these photographs a special poignancy. The artist isn't simply a voyeur interested in shocking audiences; rather, he establishes enduring relationships with his subjects and participates actively in their lives. Yamanaka has created uncomfortable but moving portraits in which the humanity of the women offsets the discomfort of seeing their bodies and faces so intimately.

The intensity of Jeffrey Saldinger's figurative paintings is created through another means altogether. His portraits are the result of precisely rendered studies of line, color, and shadow. Self-taught, Saldinger is a rigorous painter, endlessly exploring the qualities of his chosen materials, oil on linen, to achieve a seductively luminescent paint surface and an uncompromising depiction of every detail, no matter how small. By making only portraits using live models—first himself, then others (his wife, a neighbor, a friend) in a predominantly *grisaille* palette, he is able to explore the endless possibilities of painting within a self-limited framework. He varies his own representation by subtly changing his appearance—wearing a different pair of eyeglasses, adding a hat, a new t-shirt, and so on. But it is the manipulation of his expression from canvas to canvas that is most provocative. In one work he squeezes his eyes shut, in another he puckers his lips, and furrows his brow. These changing facial expressions allow Saldinger to push himself technically as an artist, seeing if he can, for example, portray every wrinkle that appears around his mouth when he purses his lips. This practice also allows different aspects of his character to emerge, and the viewer takes note of his humor, curiosity, skepticism, and passion. Despite Saldinger's rigorous, almost scientific immersion in the process of painting, a range of emotions seeps out of these intimate portraits. Because he paints from live models, each work can take several months, a fact recorded in many of the titles. Thus, in *Self-Portrait, July–November, 1995,* the work becomes an encapsulation or a composite of a particular time span. Given that Saldinger's subjects are few, he is actually documenting the aging process itself.

Contemporary western society's fear of aging is manifest in its emphasis on youthfulness and its attempts to slow down or mask the aging process by means of medicine, cosmetics, and physical fitness, giving rise to vast industries. In a century noted for an increasing faith in science and the secular rather than in intuition and the spiritual, our belief in the capacity of science to solve our so-called problems has perpetuated the hope for increased longevity and ultimately, immortality. The cosmetics and skin care industries have cashed in on our cultural obsession with hiding the signs of aging. In her sculpture, Rachel Lachowicz innovatively mocks the role cosmetics plays in the relationship of women to aging. In 1992, working with special effects and forensics experts, Lachowicz cast three self-portrait heads in face powder and hydrocal—one at her age at the time and the others at thirty-year intervals. Thus, in *Forensic Project (28, 58, 88 years)* Lachowicz visualized her own aging process through a plastic, three-dimensional medium. The use of face powder reflected her ongoing interest in referencing gender roles through the choice of artistic materials—in this case Chanel's *poudre douce rose tendre* pink face powder, the brand she uses. The result not only points up art history's masculinist perspective, but also dramatizes the role of cosmetics in women's attempts to mask or erase the signs of aging. At once funny and frightening, *Forensic Project* prompts us to examine the cultural assumption that women can never be young or beautiful enough, and turns the predominant strategy of the cosmetics industry on its head.

In an untitled work from a 1998 series, Speed-Split, the Cuban artist Consuelo Castañeda uses photography to address generational relationships. In her earlier *A History in Seventy Pages,* Castañeda made seventy photographs of her seventy-year-old mother, documenting her mother's body in a detailed, almost clinical fashion. In this newer work, Castañeda inserts herself into the image. By so doing, she moves away from a strictly analytic examination to tap into the emotional connection between mother and daughter. The work is a large digital photograph consisting of four similar images of the two figures, both nude and lying together on their sides on a white background. The artist's mother wraps herself around her daughter in a spoon formation—belly to back, her hand resting on her daughter's shoulder. Both of their knees are curled into a fetal position and their eyes are closed as if in sleep. This is the comfortable, familiar embrace of lovers or of a mother with her infant, a reprise by the two women of an earlier intimacy. In the left image, the figures are nearly upright, their heads pointing toward the top of the picture frame. As the images move sequentially across the page from left to right the figures rotate slightly, like the hands of a clock, until in the final image, their heads are near the bottom of the picture frame. The manipulation of the figures' placement suggests the passage of time and the fierce bond that exists between a mother and daughter. Whereas Castañeda's earlier work involved the artistic strategy of appropriation, here she brings the act of appropriation into the psychological realm. The passing down of experiences from one generation to the next and the process by which a parent's experiences become a key component of a child's makeup are poignantly conveyed through the simple physical interaction shown in Castañeda's photograph.

Susan Unterberg, also interested in the bond that exists between parent and child, has created a series of diptych Polaroids of fathers and sons. The portraits are highly formalized and posed, having been taken in the studio with no background or setting. Yet through their choice of clothing, pose, and expression, a great deal is revealed about the subjects and their relationships to one another. In one work from this Father/Son series, the patriarch of a black American family stands slightly off center, his figure split between the two panels of the diptych. He faces the camera dressed conservatively in a dark suit, crisp white shirt, and tie, with a handkerchief protruding from his left breast pocket. His two sons stand slightly off to the side facing him. They, too, are dressed in suits and ties, yet they appear more relaxed—their coats slightly disheveled, their stances less rigid. The siblings stand close together, but a physical gap exists between the father and his sons, a visual metaphor for the "generation gap" that many family members struggle to bridge.

"Age is something that doesn't matter, unless you're a cheese."

—Billie Burke

"The great thing about getting older is that you don't lose all the other ages you've been."

—Madeleine L'Engle

The generations of a family both mark and embody the passage of time. Korean artist Cho Duck Hyun has created a new work for *The Time of Our Lives* that is part of a larger project entitled *Genealogy*. Cho creates enormous conté and pencil drawings on canvas, representing several generations of a family. Based on vintage photographs (some as old as a hundred years) from a variety of sources, including his own family albums, the artist reconfigures the characters into the format of a traditional family portrait. The result is a "family" with little or no biological or marital ties, made up of Koreans, Japanese, and Chinese who have lived during different eras and within separate sociocultural systems. The format, however, leads the viewer to assume they are related. By representing these figures from the past, Cho revitalizes their memory and pays homage to their lives. By creating fictional genealogies, Cho refers to the traditional importance of the family in Korea, where an average of three generations live under one roof, producing strong intergenerational bonds. At the same time, he acknowledges the changing status of the family in contemporary Korean culture with a fabrication that questions the importance of chronological order and biological relationships. In a land that's been divided into two countries, North and South, and a culture in which conflict between generations is growing, Cho creates a harmonious, albeit fictive world.

Geneviève Cadieux uses the body to represent generalized experience within a cultural system. In several photographic works from the 1990s, Cadieux explores changes to the maturing body by using images of gray hair and wrinkles around the eyes. Defying conventional notions of what is acceptable or palatable for public view, Cadieux amplifies parts of the body to intimidating scale and documents the effects of time and conflict on it, particularly focusing on violations to the surface of the skin. *Le Corps du Ciel* (The Body of the Sky), a large photographic diptych mounted on plexiglass, is a close-up of a deep, dark gray and blue bruise fading into surrounding pale skin. Approximately 9½ feet wide, this disfigurement, commonplace but enlarged so many times that it becomes overwhelming, derives from an intensely personal image normally reserved for the private and/or medical domain. The *process* of bruising and healing becomes the image—the gradually changing colors of the skin, the effects of time on the shape and depth of the bruise. The photograph takes on a painterly quality in which variations in color, light, and tone become primary elements. The adjacent image of is of a dark gray and blue cloudy twilight sky, with the last of the day's light seeping through the clouds to reveal a cerulean sky mixed with the orange hues of sunset. The juxtaposition of these two images underlines their aesthetic similarities, which are all the more astonishing given the disparateness of their origins. Both images embody the ephemerality of these events, capturing a single moment of their existence. Yet clouds can be a metaphor for timelessness and spirituality, while the body, particularly the bruised body, is grounded in the earthly passage of time.

Not only are representations of the aging body generally excluded from visual culture, but people face a social invisibility that begins in middle age and grows thereafter. Increasingly marginalized in western society, older people must struggle to have their experiences acknowledged and their needs addressed in a public forum. In a culture preoccupied with youth and beauty, those who are neither young nor beautiful are like ghosts haunting a world in which their presence was perhaps relevant at one time. In *The Giant*, Jeff Wall dramatically confronts this phenomenon by digitally altering a photograph of the interior of a large library. The architecture is dominated by an open, sprawling staircase in the center of the building, a perspective from which the viewer can peer into three floors of the space, taking in the activities of the numerous people within. Standing erect yet at ease on the central landing of the staircase is a giant elderly woman, nude and holding a piece of paper in her right hand as if she is about to make a speech or recite a poem. She stands proudly in the most visible spot in the building and seems determined to be heard. Her height equals two floors of the library's interior. Several times larger than the other figures, her size alone should prevent her from being ignored, yet the others are going about their business, completely oblivious to the exalted figure in their presence. Like a statue, present yet grounded in the past, she is near-mythic. Through these visual contradictions, Wall brilliantly captures the tension between visibility and invisibility as it is played out among the elders in our society.

A direct challenge to the invisibility of elders and the loss of power that accompanies aging is Cindy Sherman's *Untitled (#250)*, part of her "Sex" series. This cibachrome print shows a very elderly woman lying on her back with her hands behind her head, her bare and very pregnant belly protruding into the center of the picture frame. Every part of her is obviously prosthetic. Between her two amputated legs, the woman's vagina is a wide, red opening from which protrude ambiguous phallic objects that resemble links of large brown sausages. Although no partner is in evidence, this completely fake, constructed woman is engaged in a sexual act. The mask which is her head wears an expression not of erotic arousal but of smug satisfaction, challenging the viewer to attempt to control or condemn her.

Historically, women have lost power when they can no longer reproduce. Lacking this central purpose, they can be considered superfluous or even a social burden. Sherman's image brings to mind the recent medical advances that permit postmenopausal women to become pregnant and bear children. The public's predominant reaction of disgust and condemnation to a California woman in 1997 who lied about her age in a fertility study and gave birth at the age of sixty-three is a measure of the threat that a woman's ability to bear children well into her later years poses to the status quo. Furthermore, elders are typically and falsely characterized as nonsexual beings, a strategy to keep them marginalized. In Sherman's depiction of a grotesque, hypersexualized older woman, the prostheses stand in as symbols of the artificiality of the visual representations found in our culture and the failure to take into account the ongoing sexuality of people well into their later years.

Since the mid-1970s, Suzanne Lacy has created a number of major performances related to the subject of aging. Included in the exhibition is video footage of her 1984 project *Whisper, the Waves, the Wind*. For this project, Lacy organized a large public performance on the beach in La Jolla, California that featured the participation of 154 women, ranging in age from sixty-nine to ninety-nine. The performance allowed their previously silenced voices to be heard and their presence to be publicly acknowledged. Dressed in white, the women progressed slowly past spectators and descended a cliff onto the beach where they sat four to a table. Drawing on their personal experiences, the women discussed numerous topics relevant to their lives—aging, the future, their independence, death—while tapes from previous conversations on the same subjects were played for the spectators above. Lacy's work has changed public perceptions and attitudes about aging by organizing large-scale public pieces that require the participation and contribution of many individuals and organizations, making the voices of aging women available so that they can be heard and understood.

Lisa Yuskavage's virtuosic, fantastic paintings of women capture another stage in the lifelong aging process—the ambiguous and oftentimes overwhelming transition between adolescence and young adulthood. In a time of life marked by struggles to reconcile societal expectations with a growing understanding of their own needs and desires, Yuskavage's women are virtually bursting with emotions ranging from indifference to unmitigated lust. The figure in *Surrender* seems to emerge from the predominantly dark gray background, almost a figment of one's imagination. She is nude except for a pair of sexy black thigh-high boots, while her hair is done in childish ponytails tied on one side with a pink ribbon. A delicate strand of pink beads hangs around her neck. She stands, ripe for the picking, among colorful, artificial-looking flowers, her breasts awkwardly full and round with large, pink nipples, her hips exaggeratedly wide as if designed specifically to bear children, her belly still rounded with childhood padding. She is beautiful and repellent, demure and overly sexual, innocent and manipulative, managing to encapsulate the many guises of a woman as she enters the wonderful and painful world of womanhood.

"Death does away with time."
—Simone de Beauvoir

Yuskavage's *"Manifest Destiny"* presents two opposing sides of the female self and body in two separate "figures." The central image in the painting is a large stone column rising vertically into a hazy lavender background. The column represents a character that has repeatedly surfaced in Yuskavage's past paintings, her therapist, taken to an absolute extreme. She is dauntingly powerful, with a stiff, long neck covered by a starched collar that reaches up to hide her chin. As seen in Yuskavage's other characters, her psychology is manifested in physical deformity, resulting in an armless body that has turned from flesh to stone. Juxtaposed to the therapist is a sexual creature at the bottom left of the painting. She leans against the side of the column, one arm above her head holding a bouquet of flowers, her knees bent and her back arched, causing her breasts to protrude and her backside to rest in the grooves of the column. Using images from *Penthouse* magazine as her source, Yuskavage set out to paint a truly beautiful woman; the result is a figure lacking the disproportions or deformities of the women in her other recent works. The two figures—therapist and patient—are inseparable, each being wholly dependent upon the other, two halves of a whole. Yuskavage's work confronts the viewer with the mixed messages of a culture that sells products through sex and encourages young women to be sexual while simultaneously condemning them for "promiscuous" behavior.

In his work, Joseph Grigely explores the nature of communication by creating installations that draw upon his own experience as a deaf person. Since people frequently rely on writing on scraps of available paper in order to converse with him, he is intensely aware of the difference between writing *per se* and writing as conversation. For his works, Grigely culls an enormous archive of conversational scraps for those that comment on a particular aspect of the everyday, such as food, art, sex, money, or, in this case, age. He often creates a domestic setting with a table and chairs as a context for viewing the work, and spends time periodically throughout the run of the exhibition having conversations with visitors. *Untitled Conversation* explores the ways in which discussions about age and aging parallel those around deafness or difference. Grigely's work is, among other things, about overcoming obstacles to communication to move toward more complex modes of interaction, particularly in relation to familiar issues.

The passage of time is intimately wrapped up in concepts of age and aging. The ticking of a clock is both a metaphor for the aging body (i.e. "biological clock") and a symbol of the metaphysical essence of the universe. Time is reliable. It is consistent. It is also fleeting, confining, and arbitrary. The Canadian artist Micah Lexier works with a variety of indicators of time, such as the minute, actuarial tables of life expectancy, and generations of a family, in order to create objects that concretize the temporal. In *David Grid* (a variation on an earlier work titled *Portrait of David)*, Lexier investigates the life cycle. The artist placed an ad with the heading "Is Your Name David?" in a Winnipeg newspaper, asking for volunteers named David, aged one to seventy-five—the average male life expectancy in North America—to have their pictures taken. He worked with the first volunteer of each age and photographed each one in black and white in the same frontal pose. The original work consisted of life-sized prints installed chronologically in a linear format. In *David Grid,* the prints are smaller and laid out chronologically in a grid. Highlighting this banal commonality between his subjects has a surprising result: bringing together all these Davids creates one life out of the lives of many. At the same time, it is obvious that each David is distinct. Lexier literally gives many faces to the scientific calculation of life expectancy, underscoring the absurdity of our fixation with where we stand in our own life span. Since Lexier is a North American male with a life expectancy of seventy-five years (albeit *not* named David) the work also functions as a self-portrait. It encourages viewers, no matter what their age, to accept the passage of time as a fact of life and to consider the multiple ways with which we document and track it.

"When an old person dies, it's like a library going up in flames."

—Anonymous

Bruce Cannon's sculptural piece, coincidentally entitled *The Time of Your Life,* is a humorous yet dark approach to the issue of life expectancy. Inside a cast-iron antique clock Cannon has installed a complicated technological system consisting of a computer, a battery-backed clock, a digital speech system, a numerical LED display, key switch, and a skeleton key. When an individual buys the work, Cannon feeds the owner's date of birth into the computer. The owner then uses the skeleton key to activate the clock. Once activated, the computer uses actuarial data to predict the owner's life expectancy. In a computerized female voice, the clock functions as a daily reminder, announcing, "You have x-number of days to live." At the same time, the owner can watch time slipping away as the LED display shows the seconds passing. If the owner lives longer than statistically expected, the clock announces, "Congratulations, you've cheated death by x-number of days." Cannon's work playfully addresses our preoccupation with death and our desire to beat the odds by continually seeking the "secret" to longevity and attempting to stave off the inevitable. Another piece by Cannon, *Reflection,* uses technology to photographically document the owner's changing features, amassing a life-long flip book of changing features.

In a poetic depiction of the passage of time, Yoshiko Kanai's sculpture *Time Grabber* consists of multiple pairs of ceramic hands mounted vertically on the wall. The hands are cupped, with palms facing up, the gesture of one who holds something valuable, delicate, yet ephemeral. Kanai's piece also calls attention to the inevitability of the passage of time and the futility of any attempt to stop or slow it down. At the same time that the work alludes to the ephemeral and fleeting essence of time, it reminds us to embrace each moment rather than rushing frantically from one thing to the next.

J Mandle Performance, an innovative, Brooklyn-based performance group, was commissioned by the New Museum to create a site-specific performance in the Museum's Broadway window. The group uses its self-described "costume-designed choreography" to make the progression of time through space tangible. The costumes are intimately integrated with the setting so that every movement, however gradual, results in identifiable changes to both, ultimately transforming the space entirely. The performance, entitled *When*, embraces the one consistent and undeniable result of the passage of time—change. The performance acknowledges light as the universal indicator of the passage of time by referencing the sundial, an outmoded yet basic tool to mark and track time. Performance is a particularly suitable media with which to explore aging, as it embodies duration. In *When*, two dancers are bound to the interior space of the window, their costumes attached to large white panels. As they move slowly clockwise through the space, there is an increasing awareness of the characters as physical beings who change over time as they separate themselves from the panels. Interested in children's sense of time, which stems from an internal clock that monitors metabolic changes, the creators of *When* attempt to recapture a state of being that precedes the more widely understood sense of time as controlled by outside social influences.

Made of dried fruit, Chakaia Booker's *Latent Prescription (Neck Fetter)* is an object that physically changes and decays over time. Formed into a thick, round collar and attached to a metal buckle, the piece suggests the neck fetters used to confine slaves in eighteenth and nineteenth century America. Booker compares the fetters of the slavery era to the youth worship of today, which she feels bridles the spirit by perpetuating myths of old age as decrepitude, decline, and a continual state of near death. With this vivid reference to society's shameful legacy of slavery, Booker urges us to acknowledge the ways in which persistent racism drains specific groups of their faith in the future; today's truth is that many black people in urban environments, particularly young black men, do not expect to live to see their own old age. Booker's work is an unsettling reminder that we do not all share the same perceptions or expectations of the aging process.

In her work *Marginalia (Mauthausen Notebook)*, Ida Applebroog also confronts the tragedy of those who were not given the opportunity to grow old. An insightful social critic, Applebroog often depicts human behavior at its worst and most extreme. Unlike her usual figurative paintings, *Marginalia (Mauthausen Notebook)* consists simply of text on a yellow background. The text, written in longhand and in columns, is taken from a page of the notebook kept at the Mauthausen concentration camp. The text runs off the canvas on all sides, making clear that this is only a small representation of the numbers of people who lost their lives to the Nazi genocide. These words and numbers alone are capable of instilling an overwhelming sense of loss and disbelief in the viewer. From this perspective, our culture's characterization of old age as something to be avoided or hidden appears shallow and callous.

Aging has been a central element in Nancy Burson's work for many years, from her aging machine to her more recent series on children with Progeria, an extremely rare genetic disorder characterized by premature aging. Progerian children rarely live into their adult years, and their bodies age so rapidly that even as children they look old. Although all people age differently, most aging is considered normal, whereas Progerian children offer a unique example of abnormal aging. Their physical bodies share the characteristics of both young and old; they have the height and body weight of children combined with the wrinkled skin, hair loss, and acute osteoporosis associated with old age. A black-and-white photographic portrait of Lee Ann, who became a close friend of Burson, is included here. Lee Ann lived well beyond the life-expectancy for those who have the disease, and celebrated her twenty-first birthday. Burson's image of her captures her zeal for life, which likely played a large part in her ability to live as long as she did. Because there are usually fewer than twenty children with Progeria in the world at any given time, it is a disease that fails to receive much public notice. Burson's portraits return to her subjects some sense of control in the process of being seen, while simultaneously calling attention to this little known phenomenon.

The work of Richard Yarde is also a testament to the human capacity to overcome seemingly insurmountable obstacles; in this case it is the artist who has suffered and triumphed. In 1991, Yarde experienced complete kidney failure after years of being treated for high blood pressure. As a result, his speech was slurred and his movement was severely impaired. Losing nearly all the feeling in his hands, he was unable to make art for over a year. When he was able to return to his studio, his work changed dramatically, reflecting his encounters with both the controlled world of medicine and the inexplicable realm of the spiritual. *MOJO Hand* is an enormous watercolor whose varied images offer insights into Yarde's experiences: an x-ray of his torso reflects the probing and documenting of his body for diagnosis and treatment; the precise pattern of dots spells out the Twenty-third Psalm in Braille, underscoring the artist's ability to face his fear of death; and the six pairs of hands are a visual "laying on of hands"—the healing power of touch, or the Mojo hand. Yarde's work addresses the fear of illness, disability, and death associated with advancing age. Though illness changed his art permanently, his work is not only about illness, but about inspiration, faith, vulnerability, and mortality.

"You're never too old to become younger."

—Mae West

For many years Marina Abramović has used her own body, through acts of repetition and endurance, to explore states of the mind. While doing extensive research into the concepts and rituals of death in various cultures, she came across the Zen Buddhist metaphor of "cleaning the mirror" for the process of enlightenment, an essential component of successfully preparing for one's own death. *Cleaning the Mirror I* consists of five video monitors, stacked vertically to approximate the human body. Each monitor shows a part of a skeleton—beginning at the top with the head, then the chest, the hands, pelvis, and feet—being meticulously scrubbed with soap and water by Abramović's hands. *Cleaning the Mirror II,* included in the exhibition, shows Abramović lying down with a skeleton on top of her, shot in extreme close-up. We hear the artist's rhythmic breathing and watch the skeleton move up and down with each breath. The two figures, one quintessentially living and the other quintessentially dead, seem to meld together into one, creating a harmony between these often polarized phenomena. Through her commitment to these ritual acts, Abramović probes deeply into her own mortality and fear of dying. The images and sounds have a meditative quality, which encourages viewers to come to terms with their ultimate deaths.

The works in *The Time of Our Lives* explore a number of topics related to age, aging, and ageism—from the aging process as it affects the physical body, to perceptions of aging in different cultures, to illness and death. Given the continually increasing elder population, it is inevitable that artists, perpetually fostering awareness of issues of profound private and public concern, will provide a jumping off place for new explorations of this multifaceted, complex, and fascinating subject.

the Time of Our *Lives*

Catalogue of Works

Bruce Cannon
The Time of Your Life, 1997–98
Cast iron, computer, battery-operated clock, digital speech system, numerical LED display, key switch, brass key, 8×6×3 inches.
Courtesy of the artist and Gallery Paule Anglim, San Francisco.
Photo: George Post.

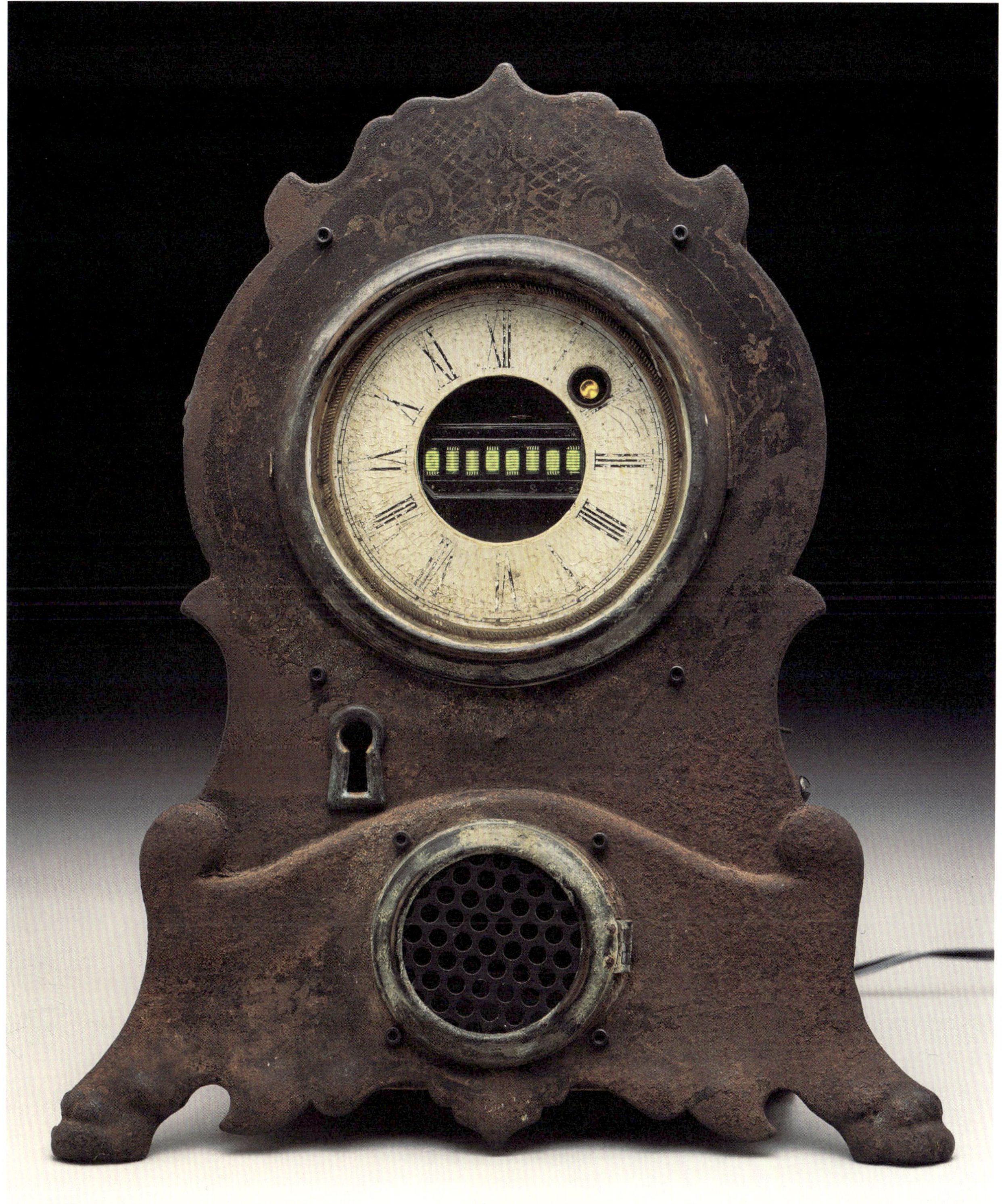

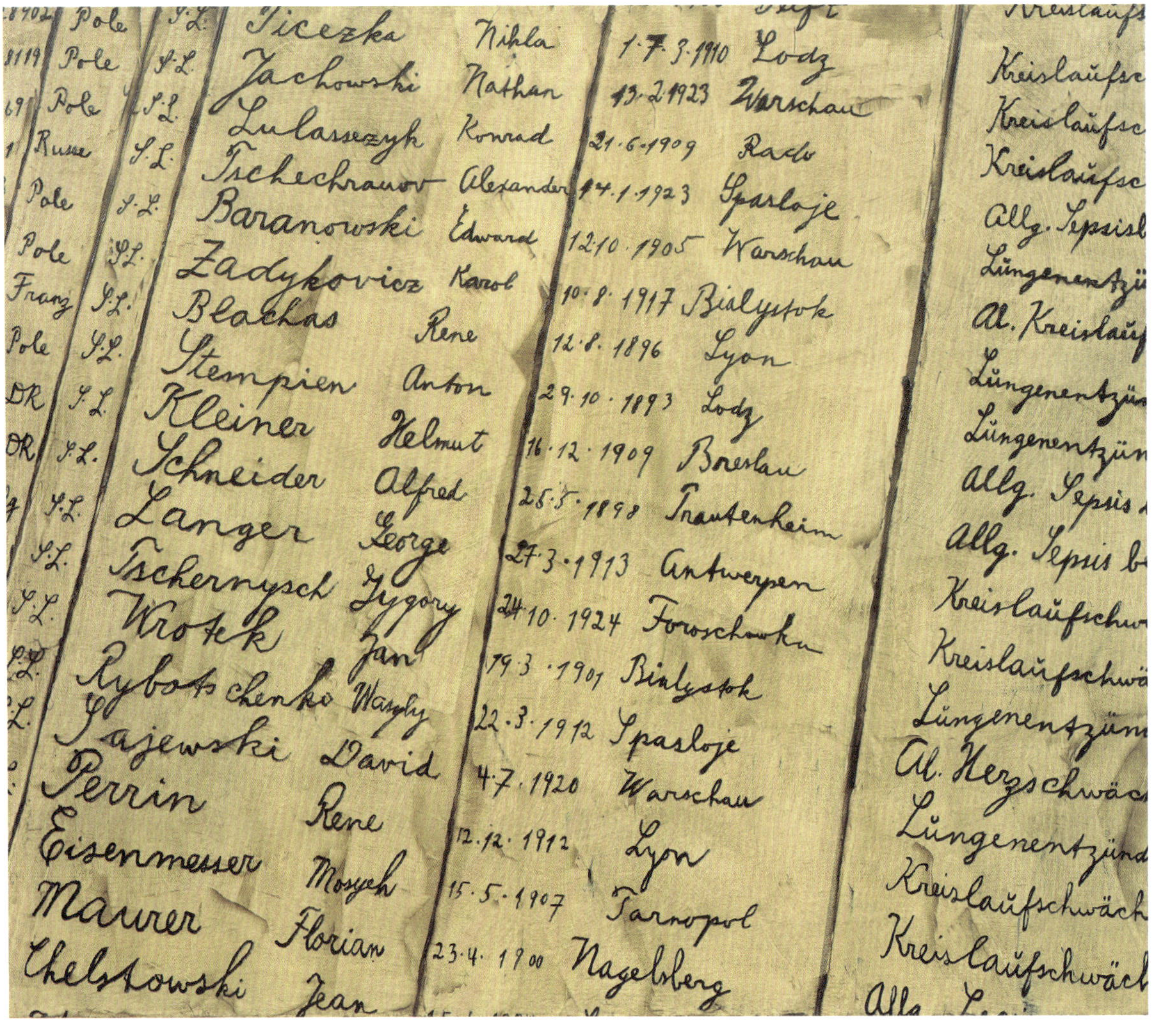

Ida Applebroog
Marginalia (Mauthausen Notebook), 1991
Oil on canvas, wood strut,
43¼ × 48 × 3⅛ inches.
Courtesy of Ronald Feldman Fine Arts, New York.
Photo: Dennis Cowley.

Jacqueline Hayden
Untitled from Figure Model series, 1996
Unique silver gelatin print,
82 × 52 inches.
Courtesy of the artist and Howard Yezerski Gallery, Boston.

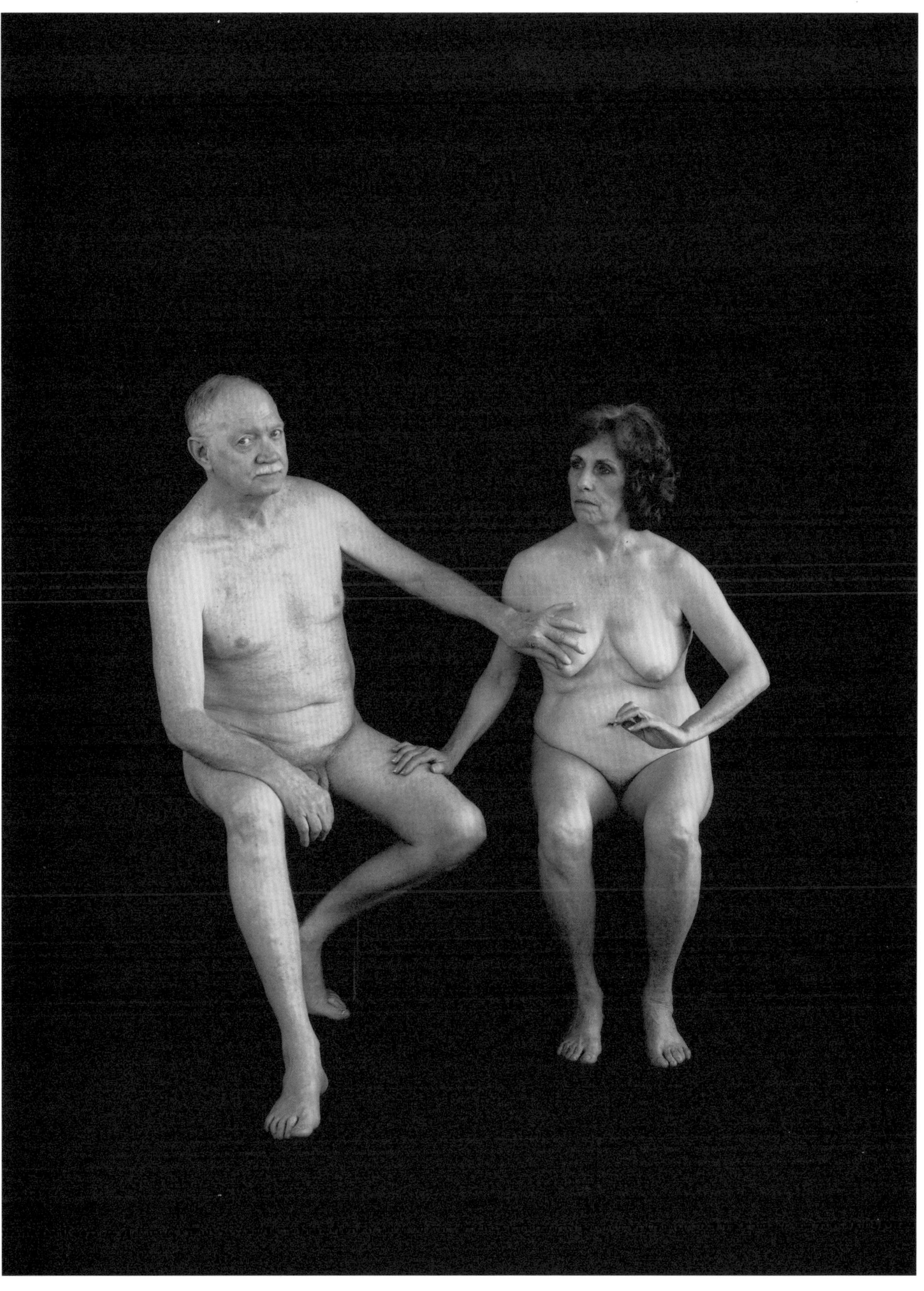

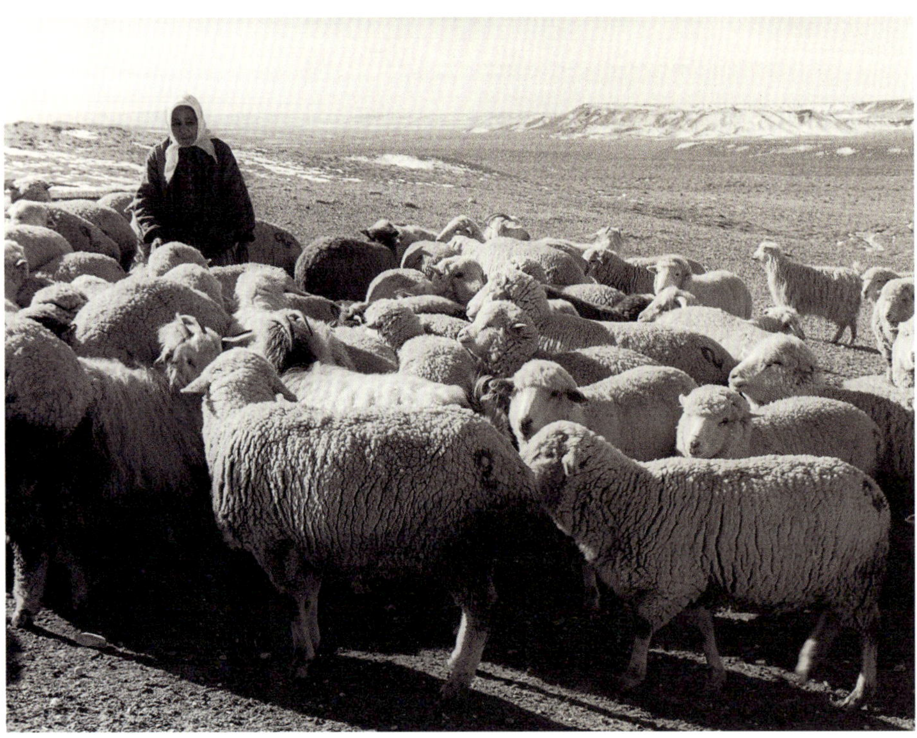

Harriet Casdin-Silver
70 + 1, 1998
Holograms and metal,
72 × 41 inches.
Courtesy of the artist.
Photo: Jacqueline Hayden.

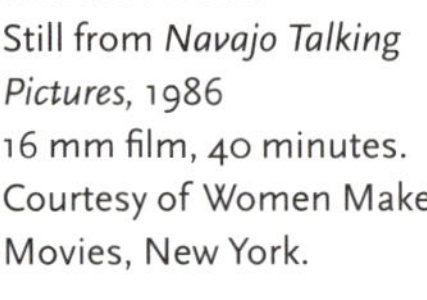

Arlene Bowman
Still from *Navajo Talking Pictures,* 1986
16 mm film, 40 minutes.
Courtesy of Women Make Movies, New York.

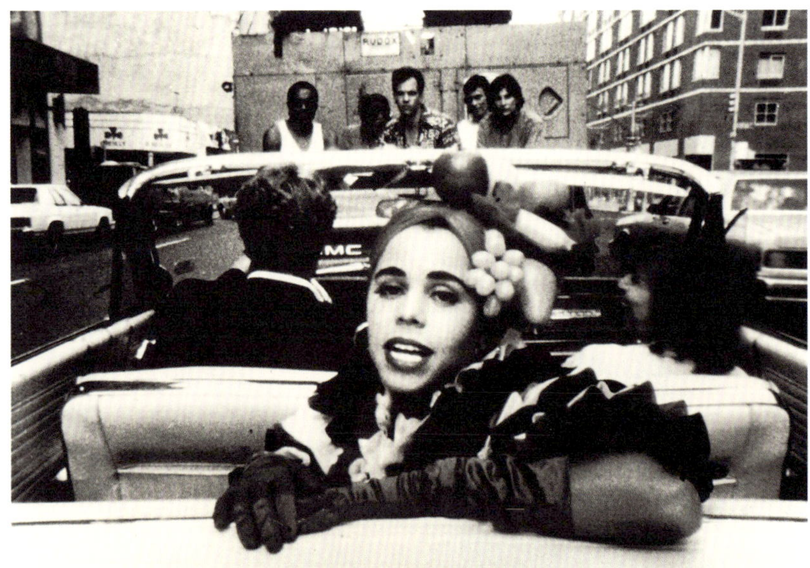

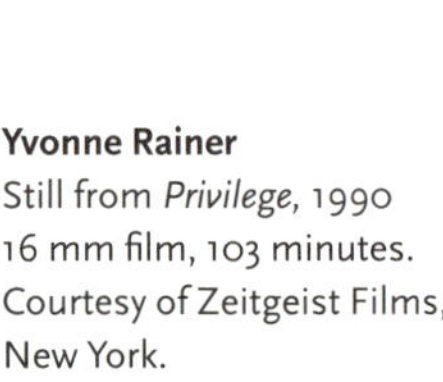

Yvonne Rainer
Still from *Privilege,* 1990
16 mm film, 103 minutes.
Courtesy of Zeitgeist Films, New York.

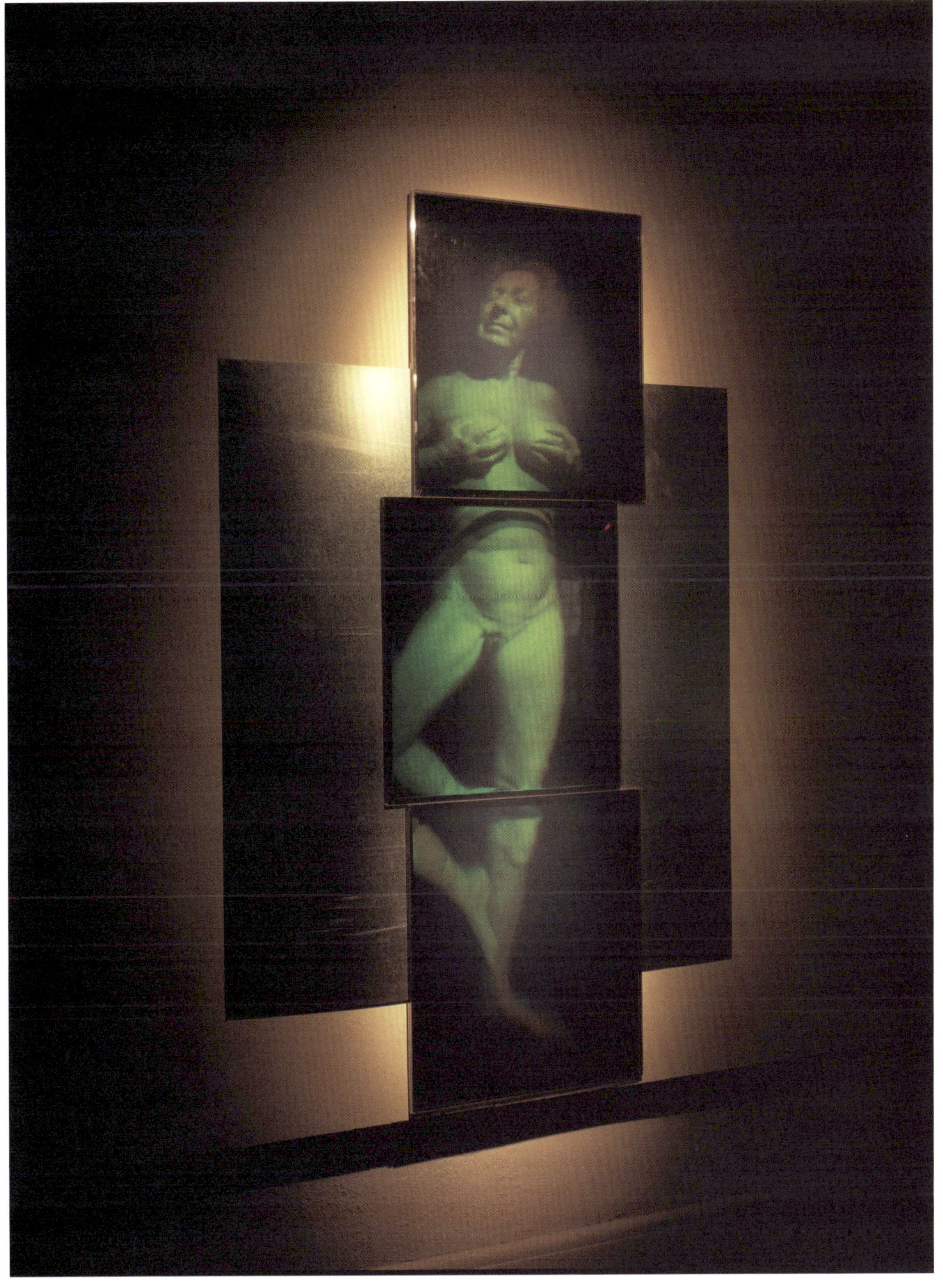

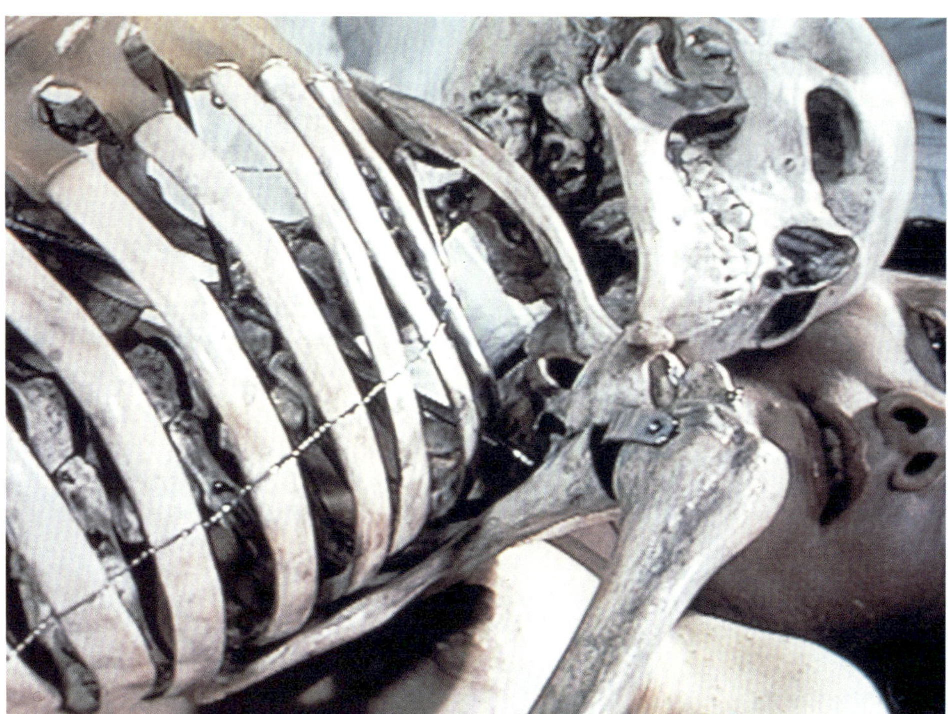

Marina Abromović
Still from *Cleaning the Mirror II*, 1995
Video of performance, 90 minutes.
Courtesy of the artist and Sean Kelly Gallery, New York.

Carol Halstead
Still from *Why?*, 1994
Computer animated film, 12 minutes.
Courtesy of Moving Images Distribution, Vancouver.

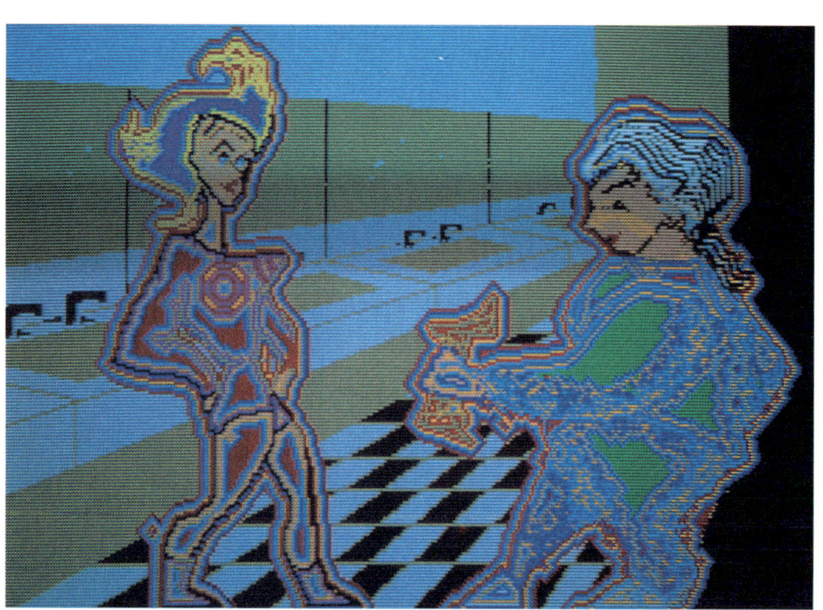

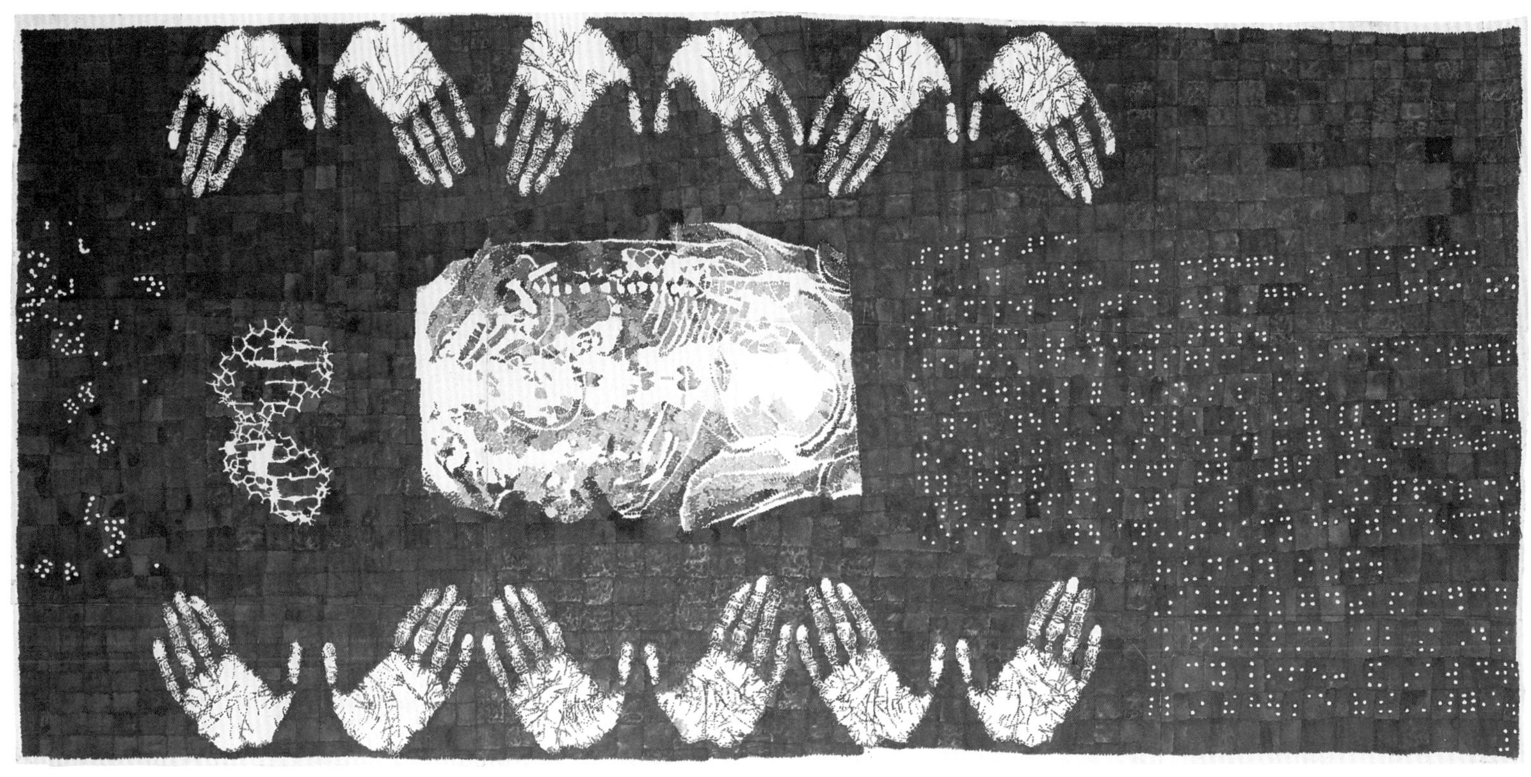

Richard Yarde
MOJO Hand, 1996–97
Transparent and opaque watercolor, 76 × 148 inches.
Courtesy of the artist.
Photo: Clive Russ.

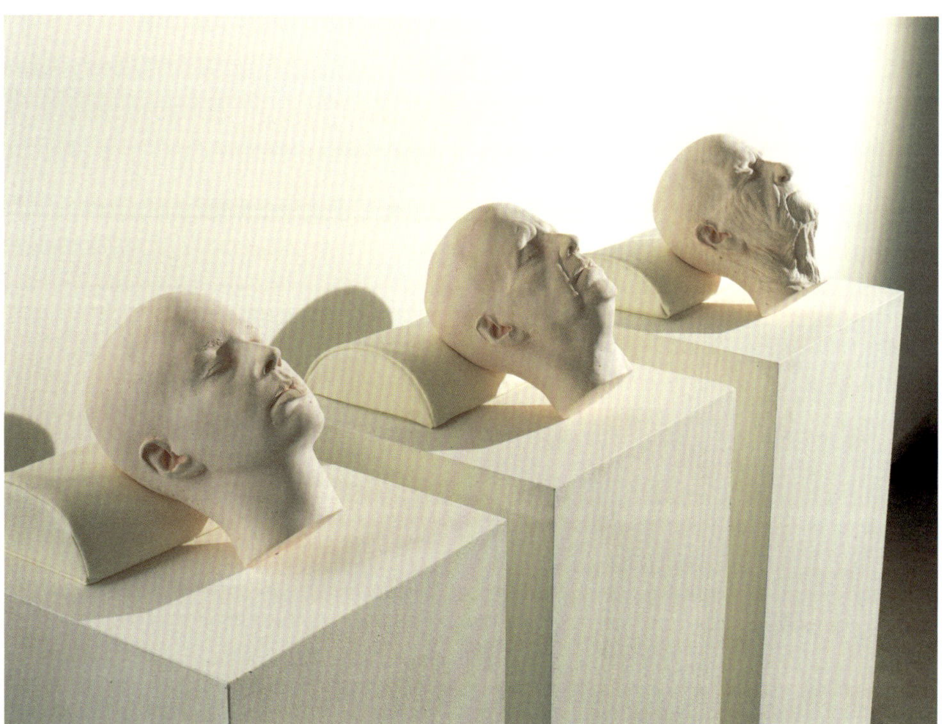

Rachel Lachowicz
Forensic Projections (28, 58, 88 Years), 1992
Face powder (Chanel's *poudre douce rose tendre* pink) and hydrocal, edition of 3, 9 × 11 × 13 inches each.
Collection of Linda Bernstein and Tony Rubin, Los Angeles.
Courtesy of Shoshana Wayne Gallery, Santa Monica.
Photo: William Nettles.

Geneviève Cadieux
Le Corps du Ciel [The Body of the Sky], 1992
Colored photographic enlargements mounted on plexiglass with aluminum frame, 72 × 228 inches.
Collection of Musée d'Art Contemporain de Montréal.
Courtesy René Blouin Gallery, Montréal.
Photo: Louis Lussier.

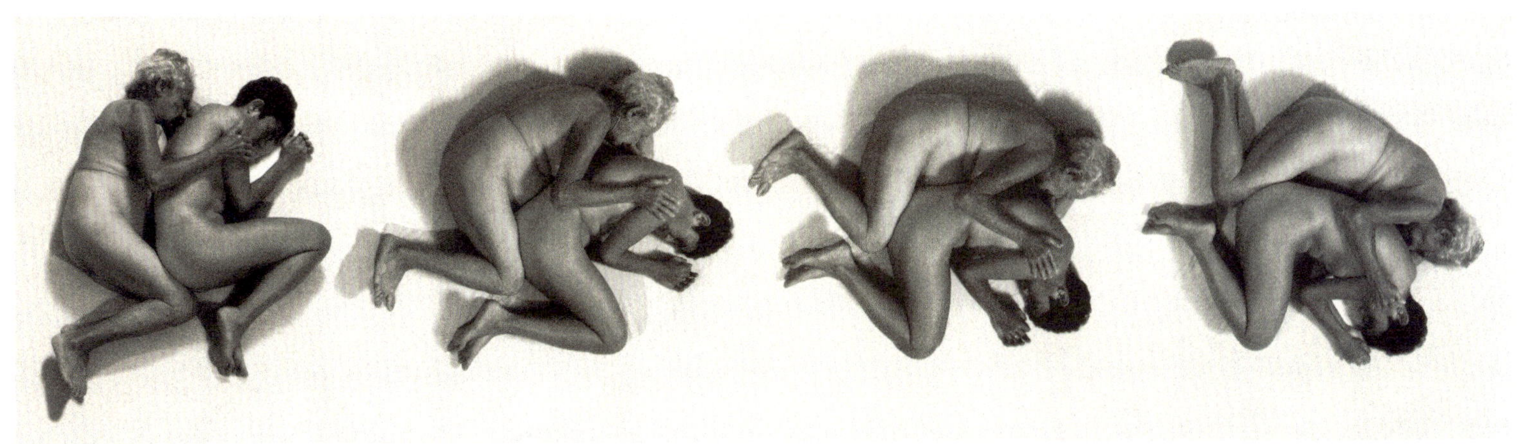

Consuelo Castañeda
Untitled from Speed-Split series, 1998
Digital photograph, 48 × 162 inches.
Courtesy of Frederic Snitzer Gallery, Miami Beach.

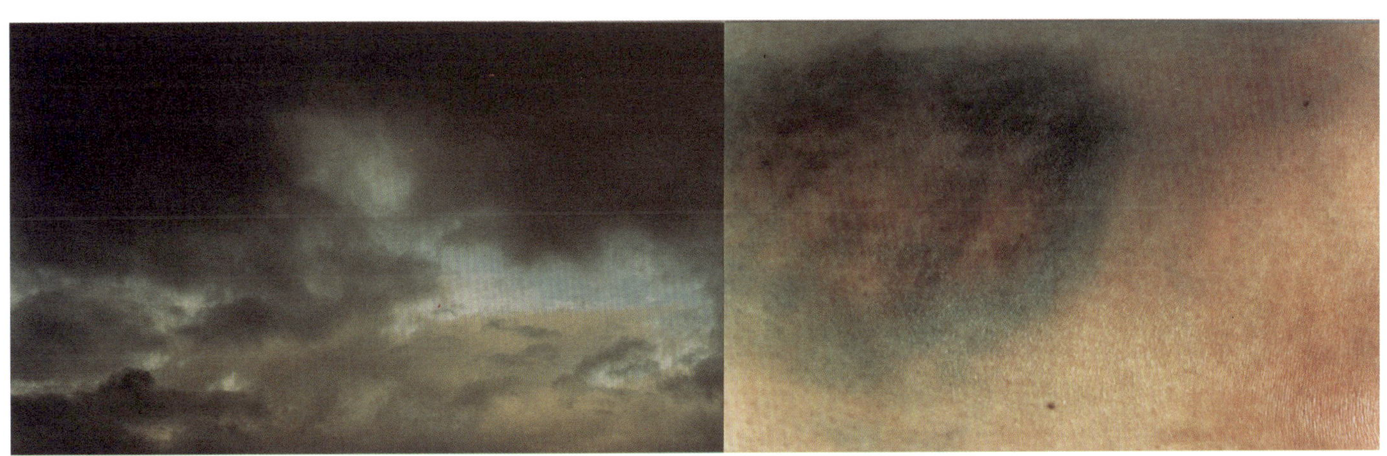

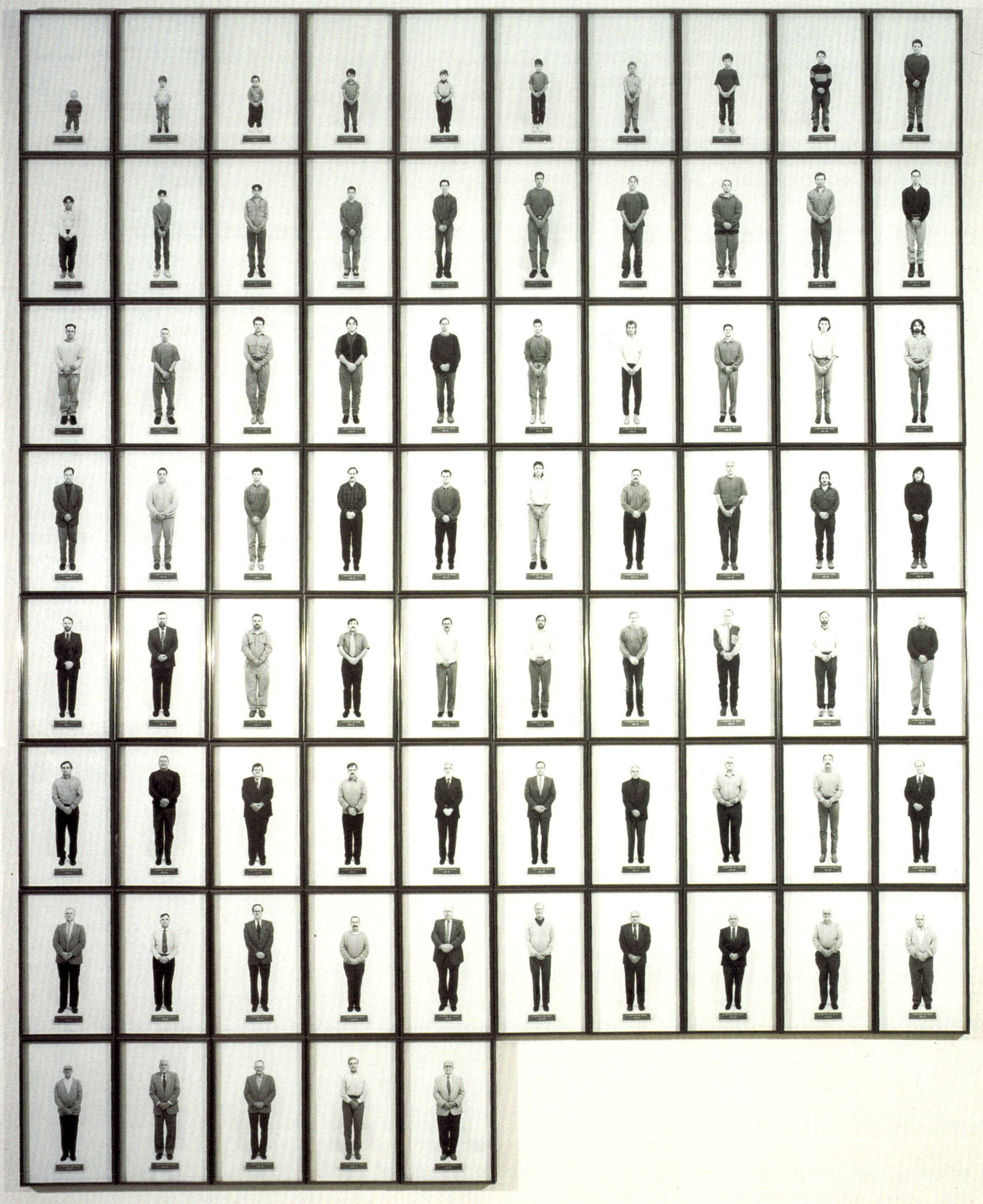

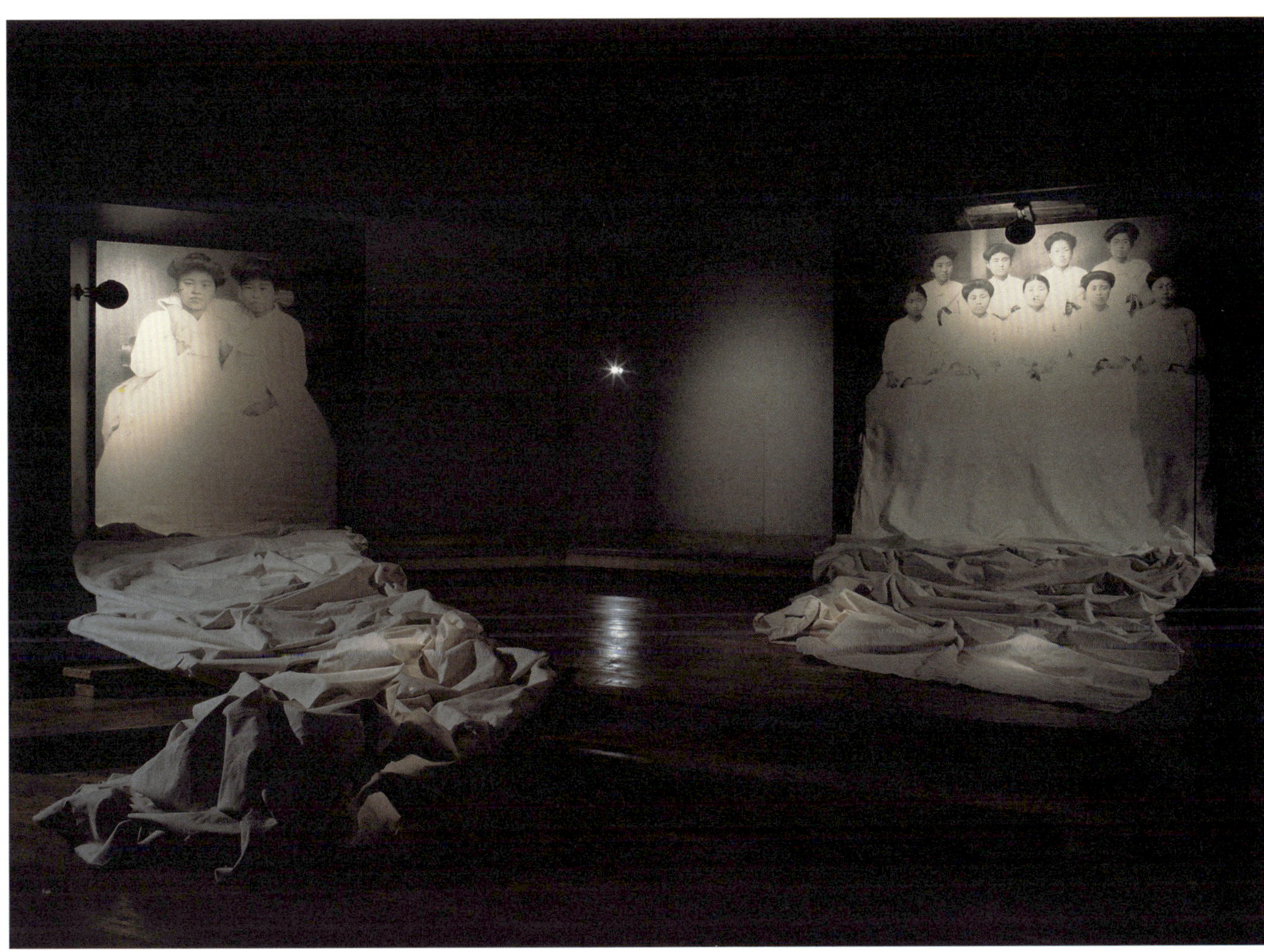

Cho Duck Hyun
Hoe-Wha 1,2, 1999
Graphite and charcoal on canvas, canvas fabric, lacquered wood structure, 94½ × 94½ inches.
Courtesy of the artist and Kukje Gallery, Seoul.

Micah Lexier
David Grid, 1995
75 framed black-and-white photographs, edition of 3, 89 × 70 inches.
Collection of Bruce Mau and Bisi Williams, Toronto.
Courtesy of Jack Shainman Gallery, New York.
Photo: D. James Dee.

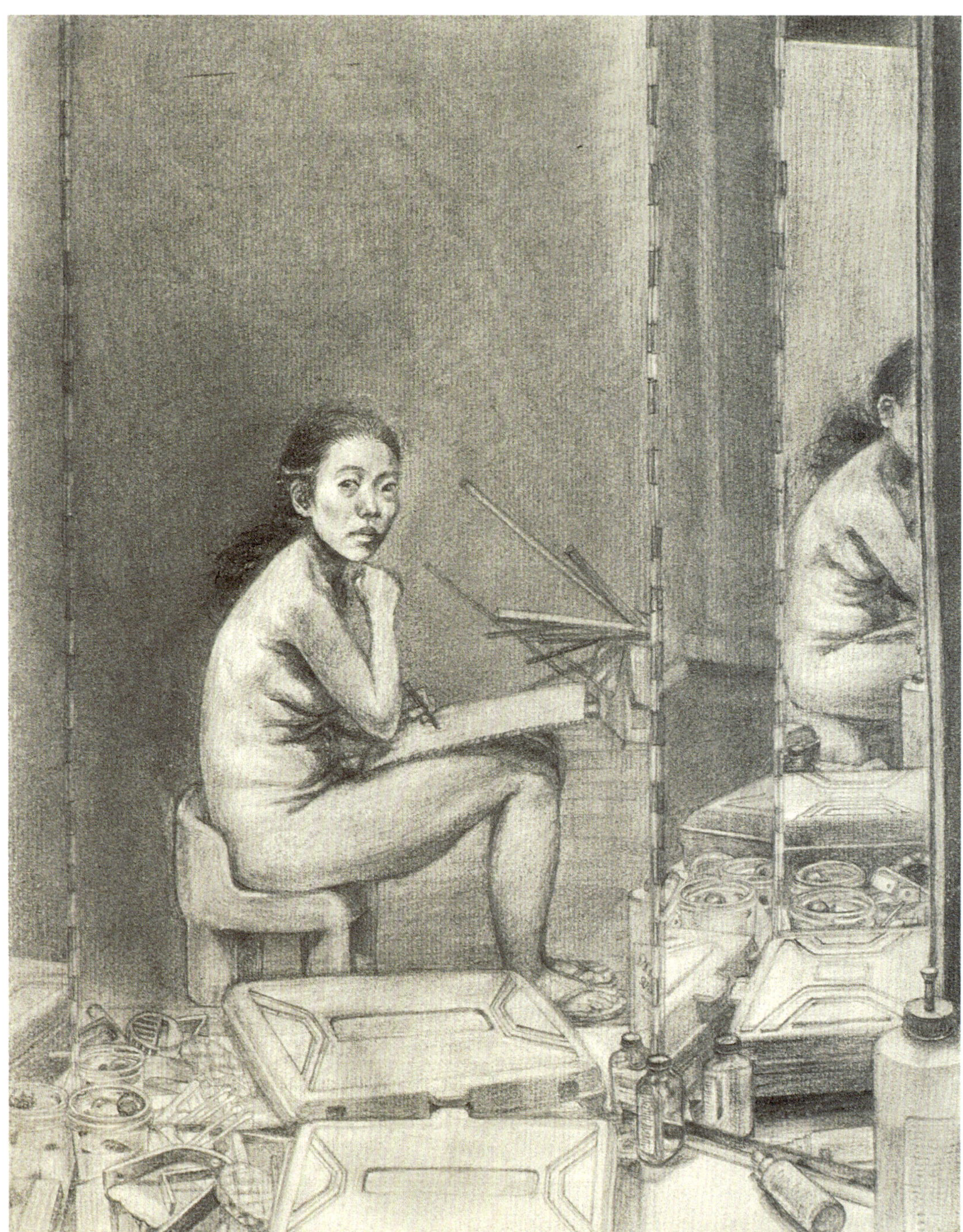

Yoshiko Kanai
In a Mirror, 1996
Pencil on paper, 16 × 12½ inches.
Courtesy of the artist and
M.Y. Art Prospects, Brooklyn.
Photo: Jacques de Melo.

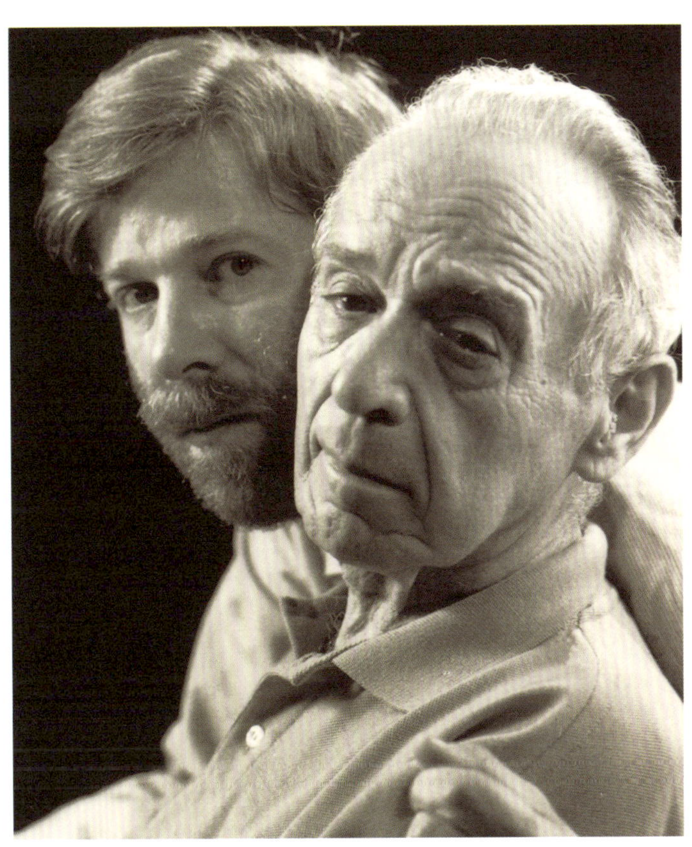

Alan Berliner
Still from *Nobody's Business,* 1996
16 mm film, 60 minutes.
Courtesy of the artist.
Photo: D.W. Leitner.

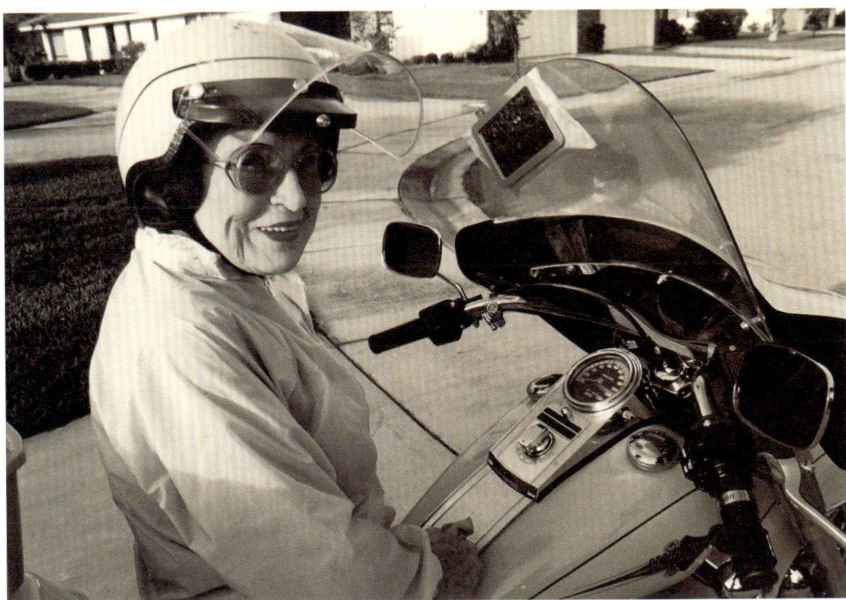

Alice Stone
Still from *She Lives to Ride,* 1994
16 mm film, 78 minutes.
Courtesy of Women Make Movies, New York.

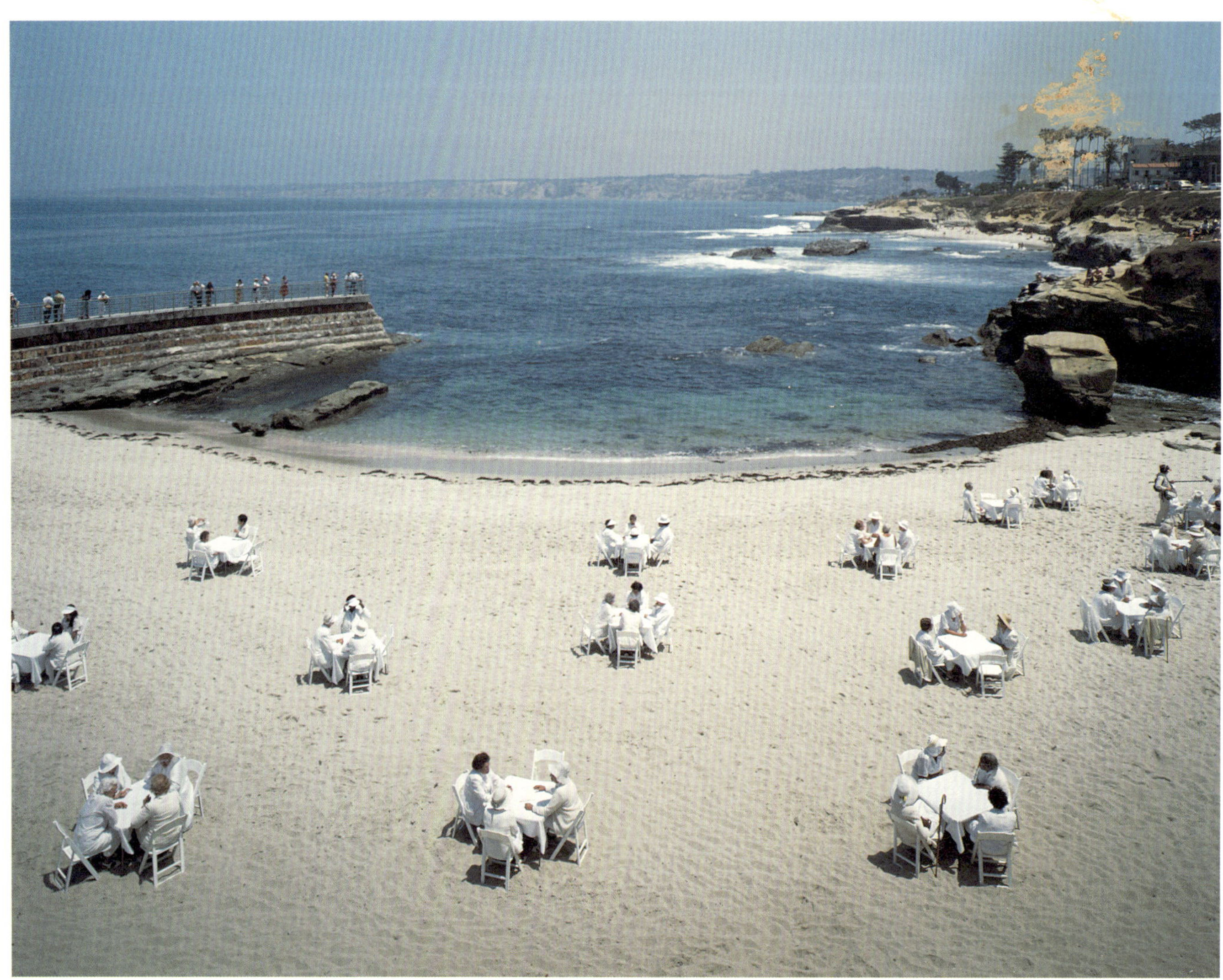

Suzanne Lacy
Whisper, the Waves, the Wind, 1984
Photo documentation of performance tableau.
Courtesy of the artist and
Terra Nova Films, Inc., Chicago.
Photo: G. Paha Turley.

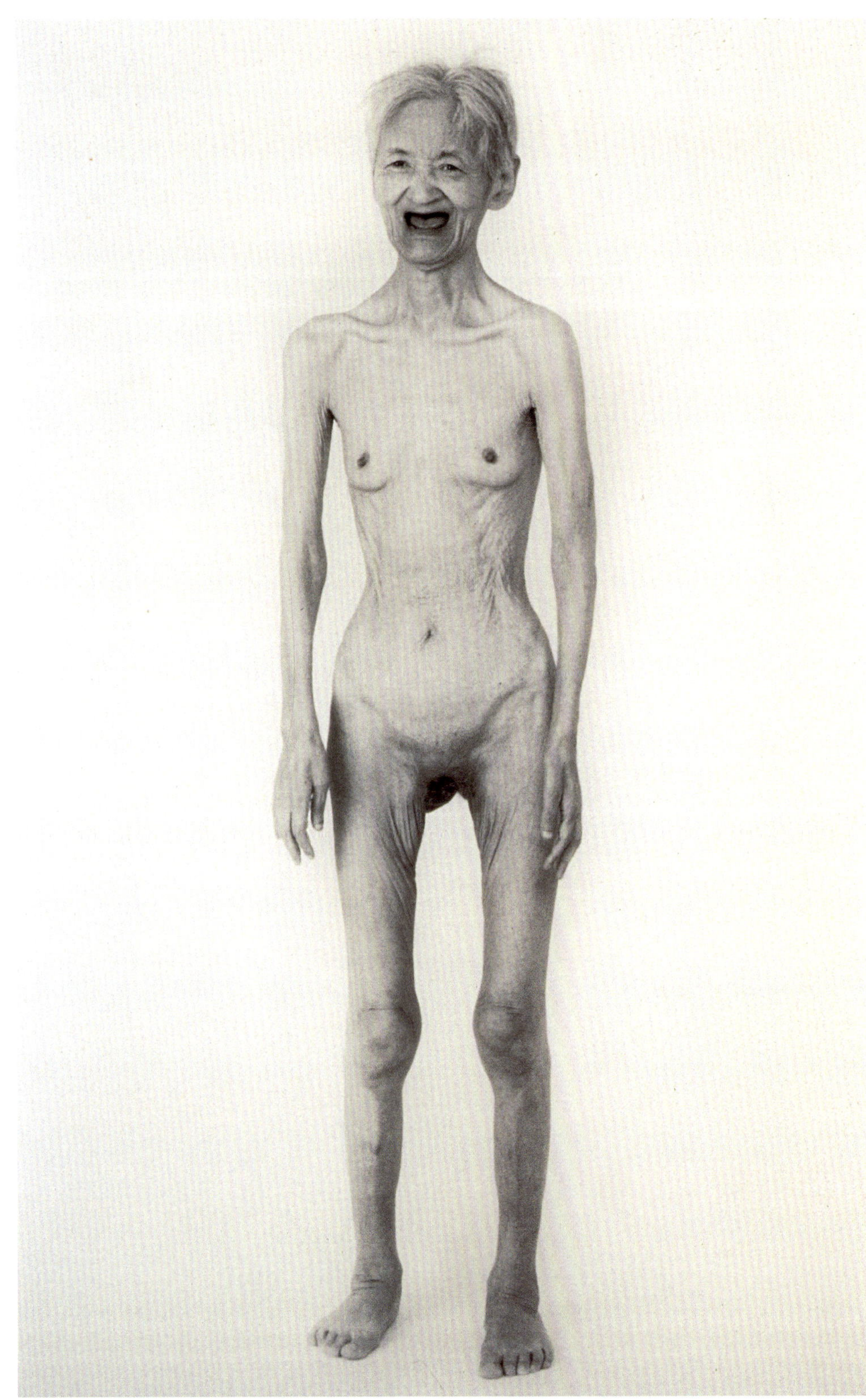

Manabu Yamanaka
Gyahtei #6, 1995
Black-and-white photograph,
edition of 9,
68 × 31½ inches framed.
Courtesy of Stefan Stux Gallery,
New York.

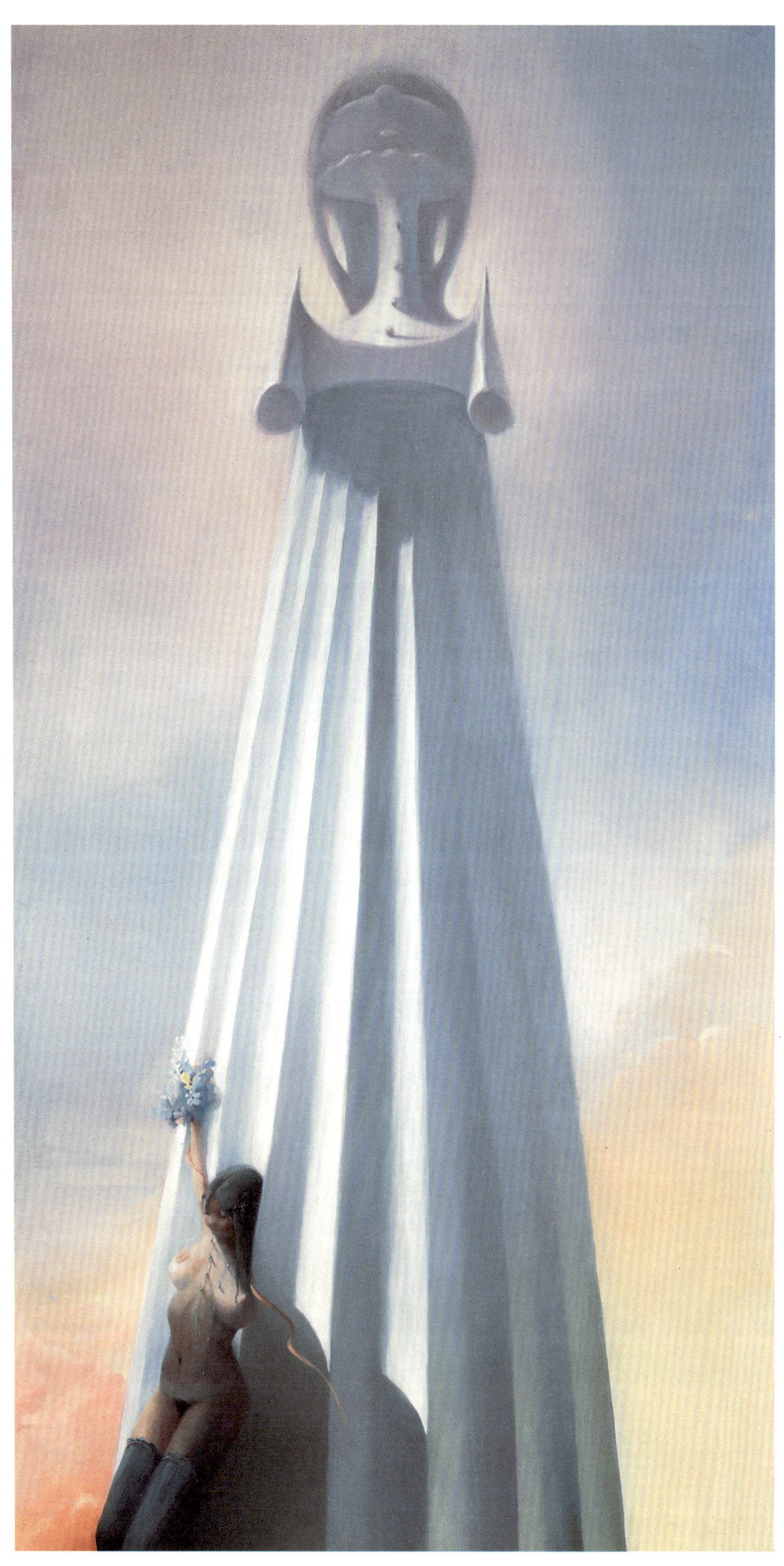

Lisa Yuskavage
"Manifest Destiny," 1998
Oil on linen, 110 × 55 inches.
Collection Museum of Contemporary Art, San Diego.
Museum purchase, Contemporary Collectors Fund.
Courtesy of Marianne Boesky Gallery, New York.

Lisa Lewenz
Still from *A Letter Without Words*, 1998
16 mm film, 62 minutes.
Courtesy of the artist.

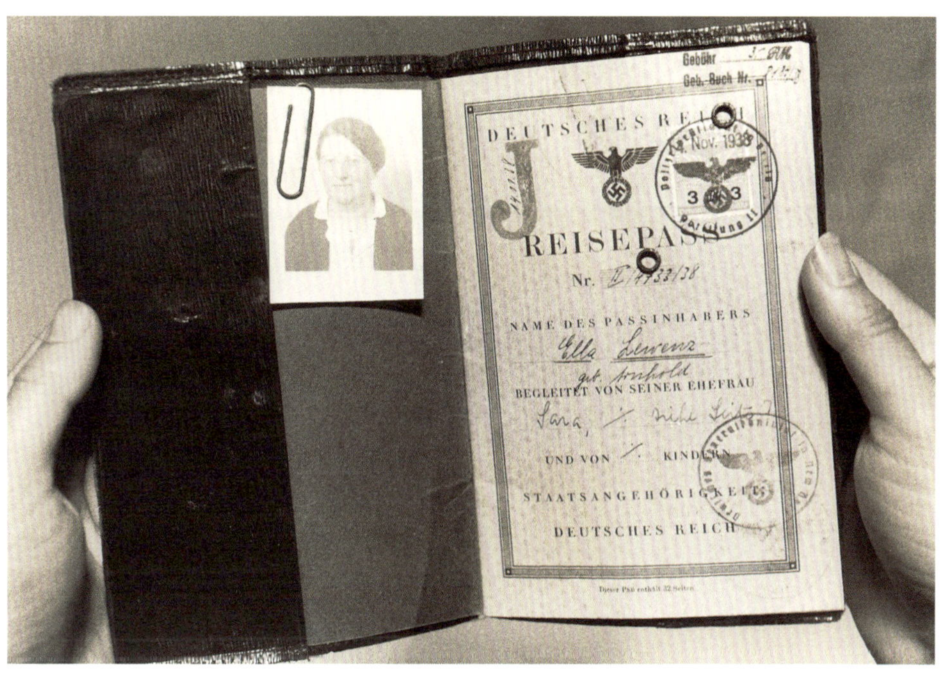

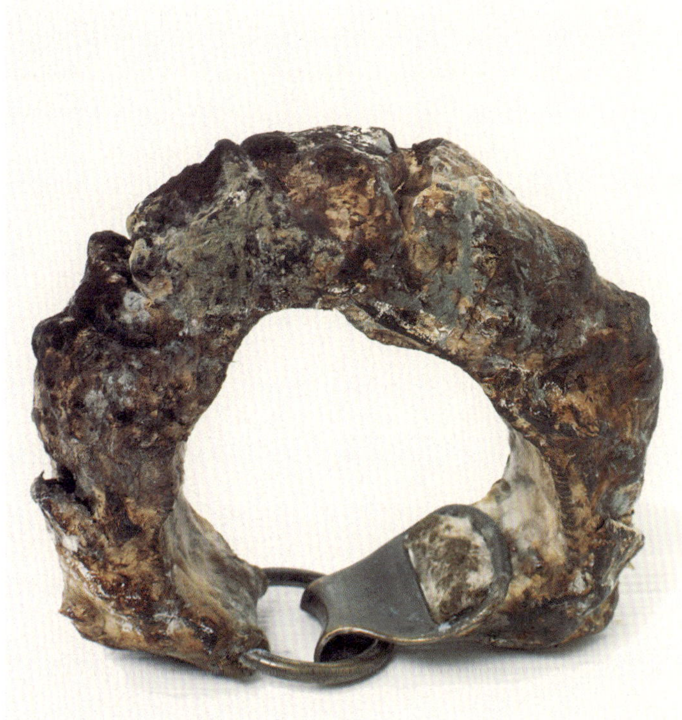

Chakaia Booker
Latent Prescription (Neck Fetter), 1994
Fiber, fruit, metal, 6 inch diameter.
Courtesy of Archibald Arts, New York.
Photo: Nelson Tejada.

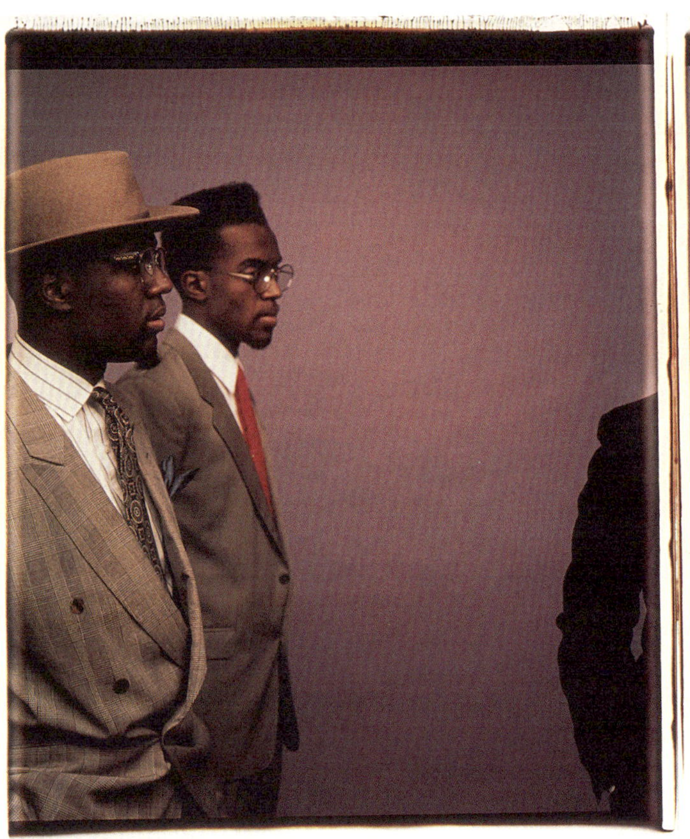
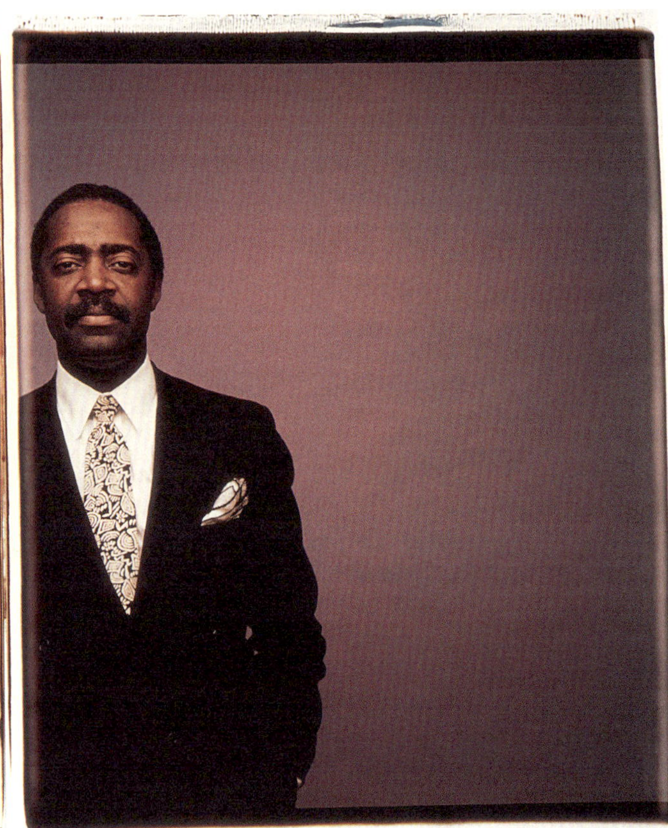

Susan Unterberg
Untitled from Father/Son series, 1990
Color polaroids, 24 × 20 inches each (two panels).
Collection of the New School for Social Research, New York.
Courtesy of the artist.

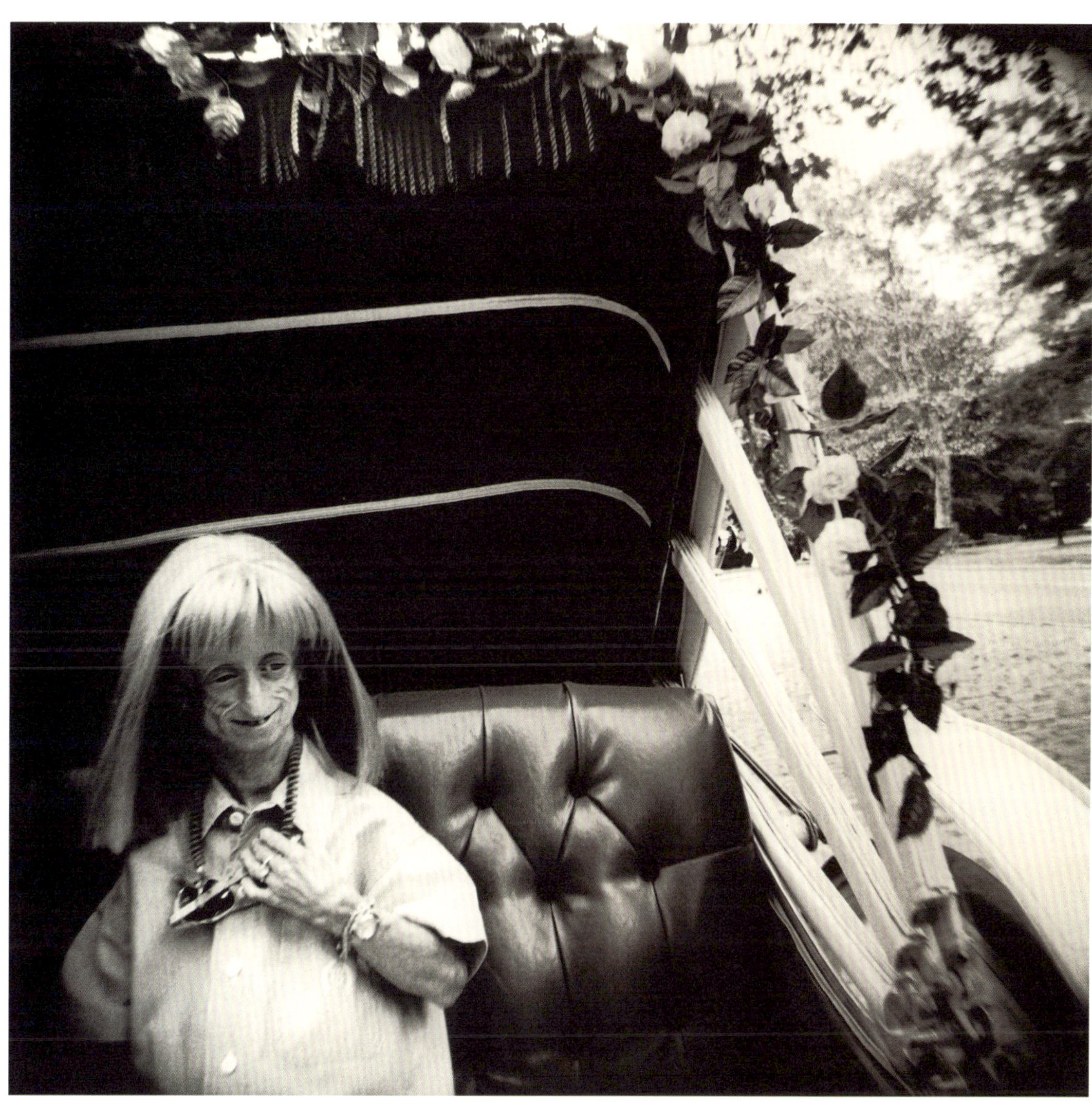

Nancy Burson
Untitled, 1995
Black-and-white photograph,
26½ × 26½ inches.
Courtesy of the artist.

My mother most
recently when I took
her to dinner
(~~said~~) was charming
me w/ her 1950's
coquettish ladylike
ways and I said
"Mammy, you are
such a remnant"
and she said "
you mean I'm a
Rembrandt"

Joseph Grigely
Untitled Conversation, 1997–99
Ink on paper. Detail of mixed media installation, dimensions variable. Courtesy of the artist and Galerie Air de Paris, Paris.

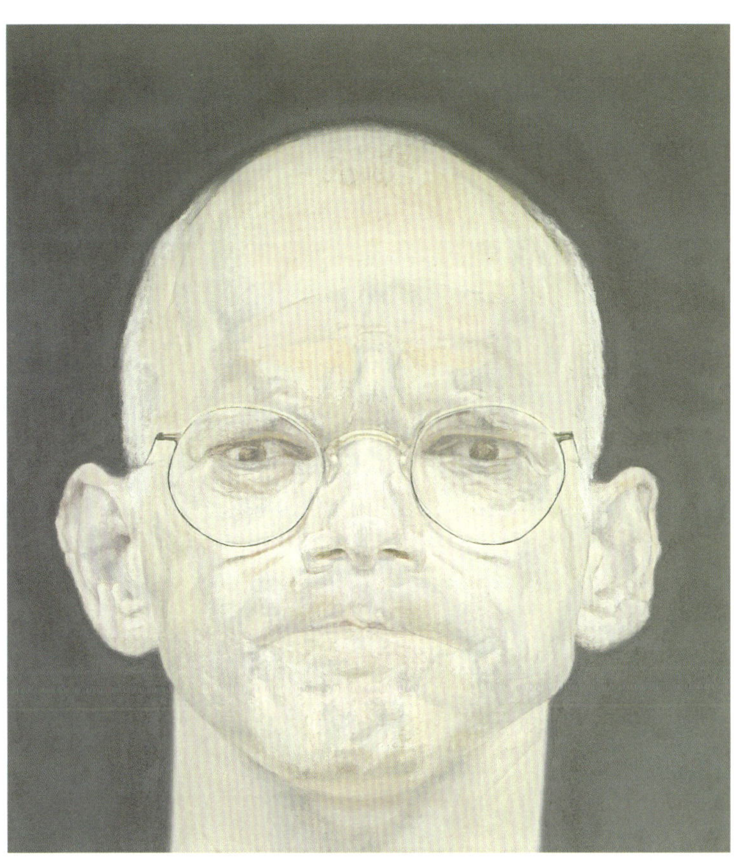

Jeffrey Saldinger
Self-Portrait, November 1994–January 1995, 1994–95
Oil on linen, 16 × 14 inches.
Collection of Wheelock Whitney III, New York.
Courtesy of CRG Gallery, New York.
Photo: Zindman/Fremont.

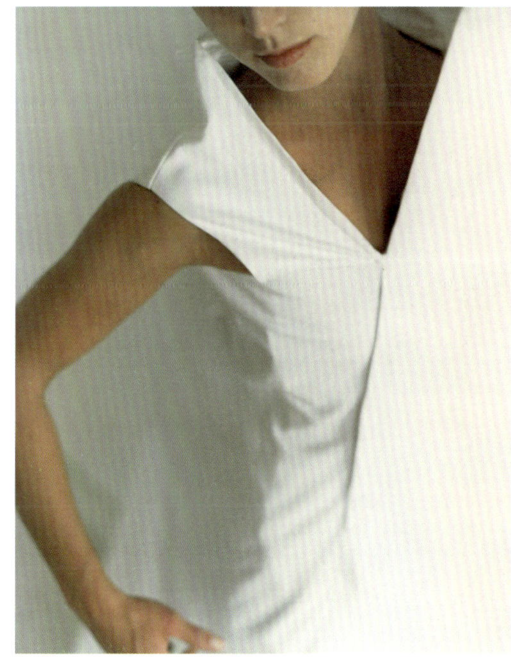

J Mandle Performance
When, 1999
Detail of Broadway window performance.
Courtesy of the artists.
Photo: Natascha Wittgenstein.

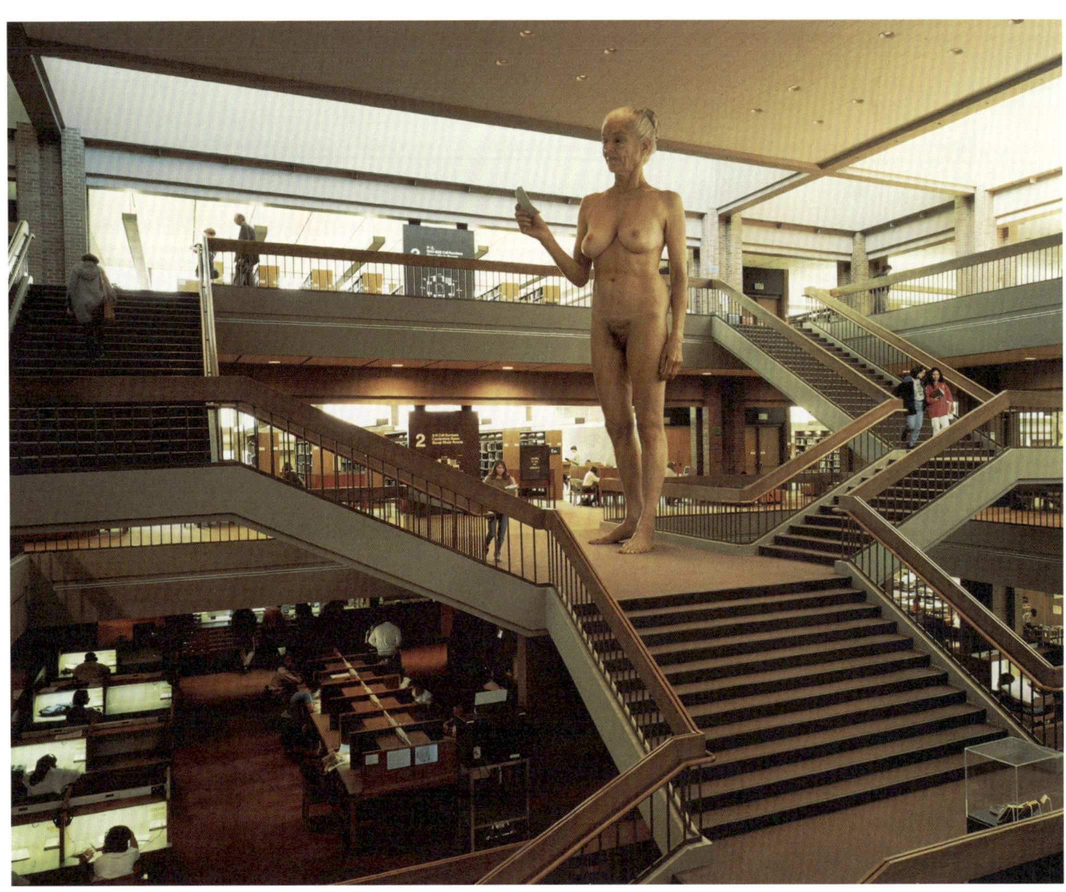

Jeff Wall
The Giant, 1992
Cibachrome transparency, fluorescent light, display case, edition 1 AP, 19½ × 23 × 4¾ inches.
Courtesy of Marian Goodman Gallery, New York.

Cindy Sherman
Untitled #250, 1992
Color photograph, 50 × 75 inches.
The Museum of Modern Art,
New York. Gift of Werner and
Elaine Dannheiser.
Courtesy of the artist and Metro Pictures,
New York.

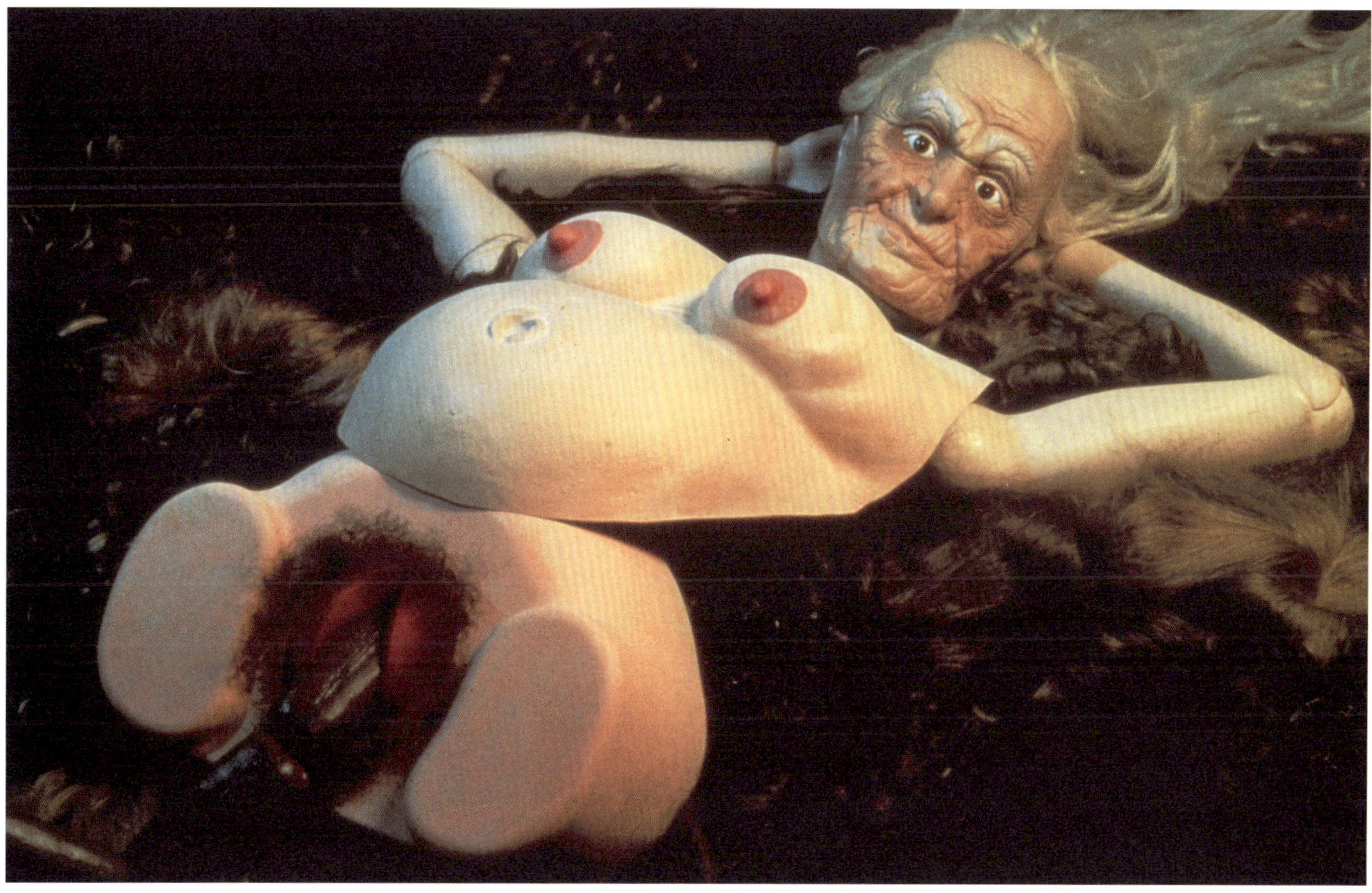

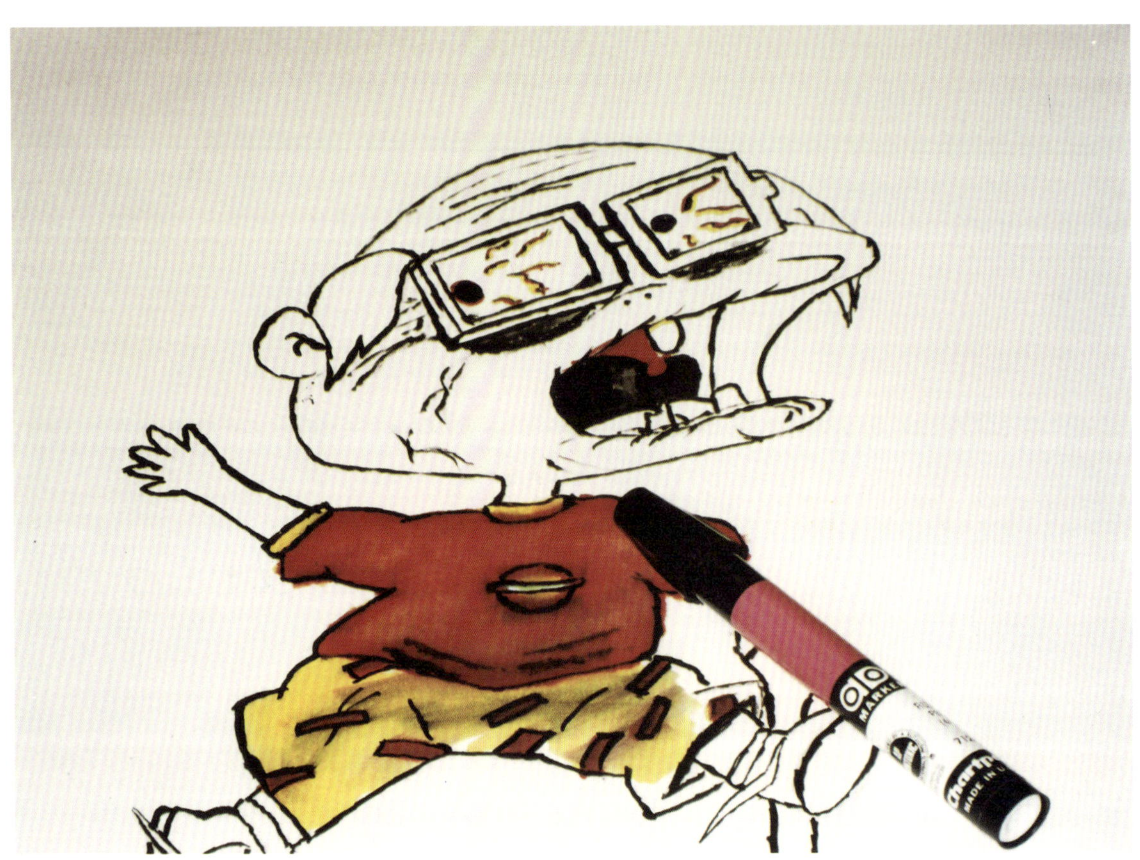

Adam Gonzalez
seventh-grade student,
Environmental Studies class, IAT.
Rugrat, Aged 71, 1999.

Older and Wiser?

ANNE BARLOW AND XOCHITL DORSEY

How do young people view age and aging? How young or old do they feel? How would high school students, young but aging nonetheless, express their views of aging through art? These were among the questions that inspired the first integration of the New Museum's high school outreach project—the Visible Knowledge Program—with a major museum exhibition, *The Time of Our Lives.*

The Visible Knowledge Program (VKP) merges contemporary art practice with school curricula as a means of empowering youth expression through a process of dialogue, action, reflection, and artistic production. Artists and staff at the New Museum work with educators in the humanities, sciences, and arts to expand existing curricula and make contemporary art accessible and relevant to students' real life experiences. Throughout the Program, students produce art, write journals, visit museums, galleries, and artists' studios, and come into contact with visiting arts professionals. As the Program promotes the role of art as a vehicle for the exploration and articulation of social and cultural issues and the themes of age and aging in *The Time of Our Lives* exhibition offered rich subject matter for high school collaborations.

The works in *The Time of Our Lives* that most closely deal with the stage of life experienced by high school students—the transition between adolescence and adulthood—are Lisa Yuskavage's powerful *Surrender* and *"Manifest Destiny,"* but even these are informed by an adult sensibility. What, if any, insights would young people bring to discourse on age? The perspectives of high school students may not yet be filtered by an adult's experience of age and aging but does that mean they are less sophisticated or discriminating? The mere passage of time does not guarantee one is more discerning. Similarly, there is no single "youth" perspective. The views of youth are as socially and culturally diverse as those of adults. Some of their views reflect stereotypes absorbed through contact with peers, parents, communities, and the media while others are astute and fresh. The strength of young people's response to *The Time of Our Lives* demonstrates that issues of aging and ageism are as relevant to the young as they are to the "old" and the "in-between."

Working within a high school curricula allows for a reassessment of issues around age within both historical and contemporary contexts. At the Robert F. Wagner Jr. Institute for the Arts and Technology (IAT) in Queens, N.Y.,

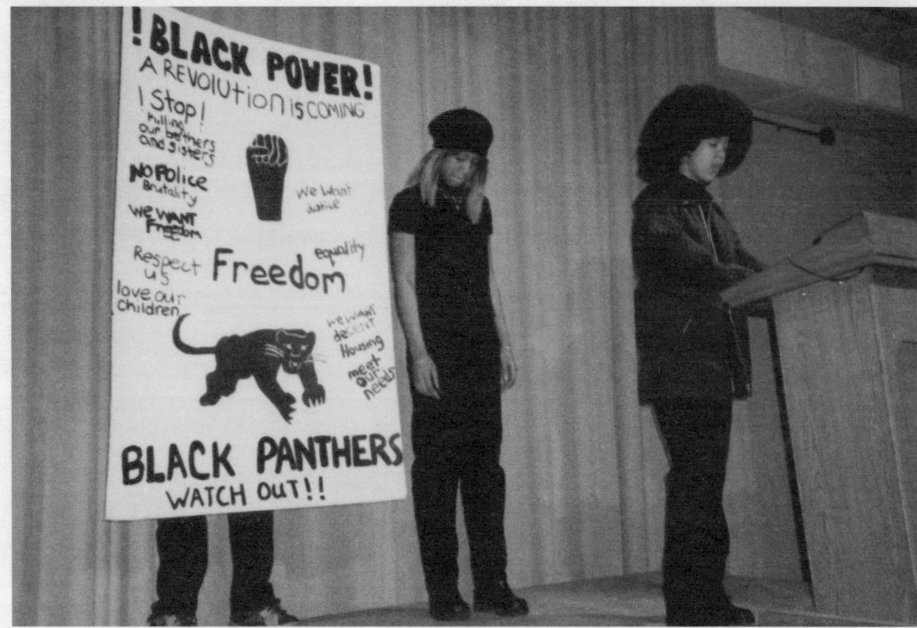

Leah Pygatt and Tashawna Jamison, high school students, American Social History Project class, IAT.
The Struggle for Civil Rights: An Intergenerational Fable,
1998–1999 student performances

artist-instructor Lynne Yamamoto worked with social studies teacher Pam Simon, English teacher Dara Winkler, and art and social studies teacher Kathryn McCarthy. The goal of the collaboration was to develop a curriculum for the school's American Social History Project class that would critically examine issues of race, gender, and age. Throughout the project, Yamamoto engaged students in slide discussions on attitudes about age in different cultures. In this way students were able to learn about history in a visual rather than text-based manner and thereby improve their visual and expressive skills.

Focusing on the Civil Rights Movement, the artists and teachers encouraged students to project themselves into a particular historical event such as the Freedom Rides, the Montgomery bus boycott, or the reclamation of Alcatraz as the basis for a performance piece. Students assumed the identity of a person who witnessed or participated in the selected event, gradually developing their characters through individual research and writing, group writing, and staging. A visiting performance artist, Antonio Sacre, helped refine students' appreciation of performance skills by looking at what constituted the emotional core of a story and how this could be expressed through the eyes of a character. "*Go into the heart of a person*" he urged, "*and imagine what he or she is feeling.*"[1]

Representing people of different ages was key to the development of storylines: "Woven into the performances were a number of intergenerational relationships between people involved in different civil rights struggles."[2] Students'

1. Lynne Yamamoto, Artist's Statement, February 5, 1999.

2. Ibid.

appreciation of intergenerational issues therefore had to become part of their historical research, creative writing, transformation, and performance work.

3. Interview with Todd Ayoung by Anne Barlow, February 17, 1999.

The second collaboration at IAT presented artist-instructor Todd Ayoung with a two-fold challenge. Used to communicating with undergraduate students, he had to find ways of discussing art with seventh-graders as well as making connections with Environmental Studies, a subject that initially seemed very separate. Working closely with science teacher Diane Varano helped Ayoung find connections between these disciplines. Their joint approach initially prompted students to research and comprehend the biology of the human body by making visual parallels between its organs and systems and those of a living, working city. The use of metaphor in this first project helped give students a more in-depth understanding of change, time, and aging.

To establish a more specific artistic focus, Ayoung explored student interests and found an unexpected common ground in popular culture, comics, and cartoons. Using these media, he encouraged students to select and "age" cartoon characters through a series of comic cells. This proved a simple but effective exercise highlighting not only the perceived value of "eternal youth"—how many of us can imagine a seventy-one-year-old Rugrat?—but also the social and cultural stereotypes constructed around age.

Tackling issues of age and ageism became more complex throughout the project, as Ayoung commented: "It was difficult at first to discuss the issue of age as I realized that many of the kids' responses were influenced by their parents and the media . . . I had to probe these apparently held views more deeply to find out what their personal feelings really were . . . even if these were still in the process of being clarified."[3]

The combination of these discussions and the art projects encouraged students to develop more complex ideas about both the biological and cultural aspects of aging before creating the interactive game included in this exhibition. The game, unlike life, offers its own rules and regulations that allow participants to age in either direction, challenging them to examine their general perceptions of age as well as their own self-image.

Artist-instructor Juan José Robles faced similar challenges at Manhattan's Institute for Collaborative Education (ICE), working with chemistry teacher Marijke Hecht and computer art teacher Meryl Meisler. Breaking down preconceived ideas about each other's disciplines eventually led to an approach that applied scientific principles to an understanding of visual culture.

The project had two goals. The first was to attempt to make literal connections between aging and chemistry in terms of how chemical reactions directly influence the aging process in the human body. The second and more challenging goal was for students to arrive at analogies on their own between chemistry, aging, and art through media other than "straight" teaching. As class discussion had revealed a strong interest in performance and theater, Robles and Hecht developed a series of workshops in which students exchanged ideas, written text, and images as preparation for a collaborative piece.

The characters developed for this piece became vehicles through which students explored and expressed ideas contrasting the "deterioration" of the human body and the relative lack of deterioration of matter. Students also looked at the relationship between the transformation of the body over time and the transformation of chemical compounds. As part of this process, students assumed identities of a wide range of characters—including those of mold and molecules—at various "stages" in life. A visiting actor, make-up artist, and playwright all helped students develop skills required to write and stage a performance piece that took place during the final semester.

The installation in the show provides evidence of this development much in the way that a forensic process documents the history of an object or a person. It has traces of and clues to the content of the performance, but does not replicate it. As in chemistry, where matter may change form through particular processes but always remains matter, the remnants in the installation represent the essence of the project as much as the final performance itself.

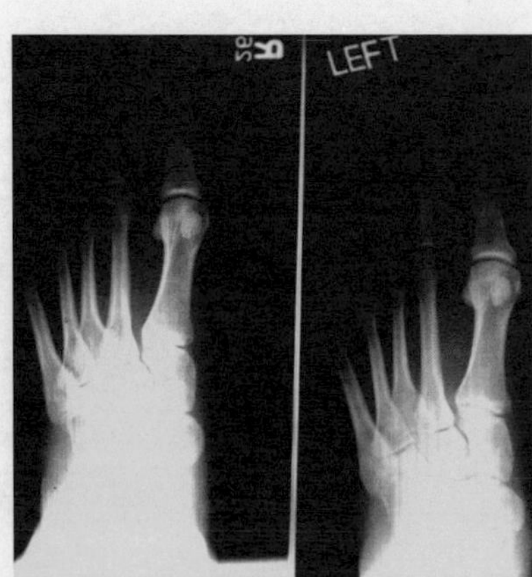

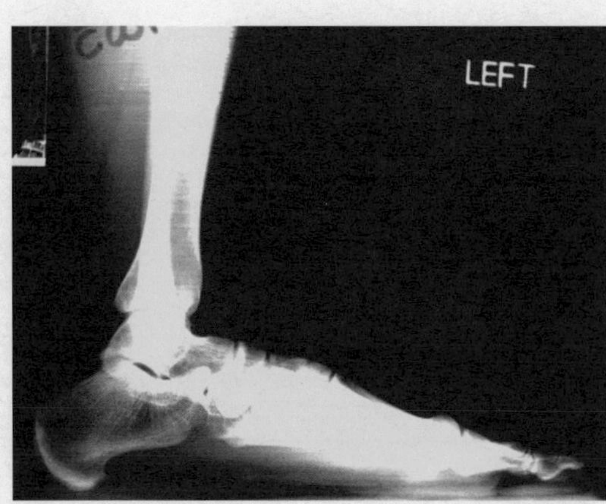

Dean Vincent Tagatac
high school student, Chemistry class, ICE.
X-Rays of Aging Bones, 1999.

This essay is only a summary of the extensive process that led to all the final projects. It is that process which is central to the Visible Knowledge Program's approach. Students' work and views are documented at every stage through photographs, videos, and journals—providing a resource to share with other students and teachers. The VKP website, launched in March 1999, makes this information publicly accessible for the first time and allows for a new level of participation and feedback by participants. With its virtual studios, galleries and on-line classrooms, the website reflects the essence of the Visible Knowledge Program as a dynamic educational tool.

The participation of the Visible Knowledge Program in *The Time of Our Lives* exemplifies the New Museum's commitment to a meaningful dialogue between art and education through multidisciplinary, interactive collaborations among artists, teachers, and students. Despite mass media and the commercial emphasis on youth, ours is a society in which some young people are as marginalized as the elderly, in terms of the often scant attention given to their opinions. In the spirit of the organizers of *The Time of Our Lives,* the Visible Knowledge Program seeks to correct this imbalance.

VKP participants in The Time of Our Lives:

Robert F. Wagner Jr. Institute for the Arts and Technology, Long Island City, New York

Co-Director: Terry Born (51)

Lynne Yamamoto (37), artist; Pam Simon, social studies teacher; Dara Winkler, English teacher; and Kathryn McCarthy, art and social studies teacher

Todd Ayoung (40), artist and Diane Varano (45), science teacher

Institute of Collaborative Education, New York, New York

Principal: John Pettinato

Juan Jose Robles (38), artist; Marijke Hecht (27), chemistry teacher; and Meryl Meisler (47), computer art teacher and Project Arts coordinator

Educational Video Center/Youth Organizers Television, New York, New York

Director of YO-TV: Torrance York (33)

Video documentation of VKP projects by YO-TV: LaToya Aultman (21), Marcin Boguszewski (20), Maude Carroll (18), Edwin Gonzalez (19), Joel Greene (20), and Irene Villasenor (21)

YO-TV documentation of VKP is supported by the New York City Department of Cultural Affairs.

Visible Knowledge Program

The Visible Knowledge Program is supported with funds from the Albert A. List Foundation, the New York State Council on the Arts, and Consolidated Edison. Teacher training programs are made possible by The Chase Manhattan Teachers Workshop Fund. Free admission to the New Museum for visitors under 18 is underwritten by The Chase Manhattan Bank.

VKP Website

The VKP website with *The Time of Our Lives* project information and curricula is at: *www.vkp.org*

The website is supported by a generous grant from the Albert A. List Foundation and the National Endowment for the Arts to provide educators and students nationwide with the curricula and teaching methods of the New Museum's high school outreach program.

***Harry R. Moody,* Abundance of Life: Human Development Policies for an Aging Society** *(New York: Columbia University Press, 1988), p. 264.*

Can we expect that the emergence of America as an aging society will inevitably force contradictions to the surface, will perhaps require us to fashion policies that promote human development over the lifespan? . . . The future still remains open, but the alternatives are already clear.

. . . An alternative scenario would envision the aging society as a society where education and human development, at last, become a lifelong enterprise, where opportunities for social contribution are available to all age groups. Instead of generations in opposition, the aging society would promise opportunities for young and old alike. The three boxes of life would give way to an ideal of human development extending over the entire life course. This ideal implies vast expansion of education and retraining for middle-aged and older adults, just as it calls for a new appraisal of nonmonetized contributions of all kinds. Instead of the idolatry of an economy based on the GNP, our public policy would be dedicated to what Lewis Mumford called the "economy of life."

The final difference between these two scenarios lies not so much in different economic forecasts about the future as it does in a fundamental question of values. Is the new abundance of life now produced by gains in longevity to be seen as a problem or an opportunity? Are younger and older generations simply interest groups, or are all generations bound in obligations toward a common good? To insist that the future remains open is to insist that human beings have in their power the capacity to act, on whatever scale, and to move toward an abundance of life shared by all generations.

Linda Cool and Justine McCabe, "The 'Scheming Hag' and the 'Dear Old Thing': The Anthropology of Aging Women," in* Growing Old in Different Societies, *ed. Jay Sokolovsky *(Acton, Mass.: Copley Publishing Group, 1987), pp. 58–59.*

Depressions in middle-aged women are due to their lack of important roles and subsequent loss of self-esteem rather than hormonal changes of menopause . . . In contrast to the experiences of American postmenopausal women . . . [is] the situation of Indian Rajput women, for whom menopause marks the end of *purdah* and the beginning of a freedom and power previously unknown to them.

***Leonard Hayflick, Ph.D.,* How and Why We Age** *(New York: Ballantine Books, 1994), pp. 17–18, 35.*

. . . [A]ll of your molecules . . . are composed of more fundamental units called atoms, most of which have been the same since our planet formed. You and I simply represent unique rearrangements of ancient atoms that are themselves billions of years old. We are really composed of billion-year-old atoms; we might actually claim to be immortal!

. . . The atoms in our bodies may have been part of the body of someone else long since dead. This is the only scientific basis for believing that we, the living, represent a form of reincarnation. When we die our atoms will dissipate into the environment, and some, perhaps, will become part of another human in a continuing pattern of recycling atoms. You could argue that this is scientific evidence for life after death; our atoms are immortal but we, as individuals, are not.

. . . Life is a continuum and does not begin or end at some arbitrary point. Despite the belief of some people that life begins at conception, all life, including human life, actually never ends...[Our] germ plasma (the source of sperm and eggs) is immortal. If it weren't immortal, we would not be here to discuss the matter.

***Bill Bytheway,* Ageism** *(Philadelphia: Open University Press, 1995), pp. 124–125.*

In our article on defining ageism (Bytheway and Johnson 1990), we put forward four suggestions for anti-ageist action. First, we should abandon ageist language. In particular, we should abandon the word 'elderly' and begin to use a relative rather than an absolute age vocabulary. In March 1993, I spent an hour expounding the argument against 'elderly' and 'old age' to a group of 21 students from eleven different countries who were attending a short course in social gerontology at the International Institute of Ageing in Malta. They quickly agreed that there was no point at which someone became elderly and that this invalidated categorizations of people as elderly. They were reluctant, however, to let go of the word itself. They recognized that the alternative *older* was relative, was not exclusionary, did not set people apart, but they wanted to retain 'elderly.' 'People get grey hair, they are more frail, they need services, we need a name for it,' one said.

***Lewis Carroll, "You Are Old, Father William," from* Alice's Adventures in Wonderland.**

You Are Old, Father William

"You are old, Father William," the young man said,
And your hair has become very white;
and yet you incessantly stand on your head—
Do you think, at your age, it is right?"

"In my youth," Father William replied to his son,
"I feared it might injure the brain;
But, now that I'm perfectly sure I have none,
Why, I do it again and again."

"You are old," said the youth, "as I mentioned before,
And have grown most uncommonly fat;
Yet you turned a back-somersault in at the door—
Pray, what is the reason for that?"

"In my youth," said the sage, as he shook his grey locks,
I kept all my limbs very supple
By the use of this ointment—one shilling the box—
Allow me to sell you a couple?"

"You are old," said the youth, "and your jaws are too weak
For anything tougher than suet;
Yet you finished the goose, with the bones and the beak—
Pray, how did you manage to do it?"

"In my youth," said his father, "I took to the law,
And argued each case with my wife;
And the muscular strength, which it gave to my jaw,
Has lasted the rest of my life."

"You are old," said the youth, "one would hardly suppose
That your eye was as steady as ever;
Yet you balanced an eel on the end of your nose—
What made you so awfully clever?"

"I have answered three questions, and that is enough,"
Said his father, "don't give yourself airs!
Do you think I can listen all day to such stuff?
Be off, or I'll kick you downstairs!"

Exhibition Checklist

PAINTINGS, DRAWINGS, INSTALLATIONS, PHOTOGRAPHS

Marina Abramović

Cleaning the Mirror II, 1995
Performance on 12-inch laser disk edition of 3, 2 AP's (1/3)
90:00 minutes
Courtesy of the artist and Sean Kelly Gallery, New York

Ida Applebroog

Marginalia (Mauthausen Notebook), 1991
Oil on canvas, wood strut
43¼×48×3⅛ inches
Courtesy of Ronald Feldman Fine Arts, New York

Chakaia Booker

Latent Prescription (Neck Fetter), 1994
Fiber, fruit, metal
6 inch diameter
Courtesy of Archibald Arts, New York

Nancy Burson

Untitled, 1995
Black-and-white photograph
26½×26½ inches
Courtesy of the artist

Untitled, 1991
Black-and-white photograph
15¼×15¼ inches
Courtesy of the artist

Untitled, 1992
Black-and-white photograph
15¼×15¼ inches
Courtesy of the artist

Geneviève Cadieux

Le Corps du Ciel [The Body of the Sky], 1992
Colored photographic enlargements mounted on plexiglass with aluminum frame
72×228 inches
Collection of the Musée d'Art Contemporain de Montréal
Courtesy of René Blouin Gallery, Montréal

Bruce Cannon

The Time of Your Life, 1997–98
Cast iron, computer, battery-operated clock, digital speech system, numerical LED display, key switch, brass key
8×6×3 inches
Courtesy of the artist and Gallery Paule Anglim, San Francisco

Reflection, 1999
Picture frame, video display, video camera, microcontroller
16×12×4 inches
Courtesy of the artist and Gallery Paule Anglim, San Francisco

Harriet Casdin-Silver

70 + 1, 1998
Holograms and metal
72×41 inches
Courtesy of the artist

Consuelo Castañeda

Untitled from Speed-Split series, 1998
Digital photograph
48×162 inches
Courtesy of Frederic Snitzer Gallery, Miami Beach

Cho Duck Hyun

Hoe-Wha 4, 1999
Graphite, charcoal, and acrylic on canvas, fabric
130×103½×39⅓ inches
Courtesy of the artist and Kukje Gallery, Seoul

Joseph Grigely

Untitled Conversation, 1997–99
Mixed media installation
Dimensions variable
Courtesy of the artist and Galerie Air de Paris, Paris

Jacqueline Hayden

Untitled from Figure Model series, 1996
Unique silver gelatin print
82×52 inches
Courtesy of the artist and Howard Yezerski Gallery, Boston

Yoshiko Kanai

Time Grabber, 1998
Ceramic
Dimensions variable
Courtesy of the artist
Supported by Ruth Kohler

In a Mirror, 1996
Pencil on paper
16×12½ inches
Courtesy of the artist and M.Y. Art Prospects, Brooklyn

Wild Woman, 1997
Pencil on paper
14×17 inches
Courtesy of the artist and M.Y. Art Prospects, Brooklyn

Touch (Dress), 1997
Pencil on paper
12½×16 inches
Courtesy of the artist and M.Y. Art Prospects, Brooklyn

Rachel Lachowicz

Forensic Projection (28, 58, 88 Years), 1992
Face powder (Chanel's *poudre douce rose tendre* pink) and hydrocal, edition of 3
9×11×13 inches each
Collection of Linda Bernstein and Tony Rubin, Los Angeles. Courtesy of Shoshana Wayne Gallery, Santa Monica

Micah Lexier

David Grid, 1995
75 framed black-and-white photographs, edition of 3
89×70 inches
Collection of Bruce Mau and Bisi Williams, Toronto. Courtesy of Jack Shainman Gallery, New York

Self-portrait as a Lucite cube divided proportionally between a (red) volume representing life lived and a (clear) volume representing life to come, based on statistical life expectancy, 1995
Lucite
6×6×6 inches
Collection of Bradley J. Currie, Toronto. Courtesy of Jack Shainman Gallery, New York

Jeffrey Saldinger

Self-Portrait, April-June, 1997, 1997
Oil on linen
14×16 inches
Courtesy of the artist and CRG Gallery, New York

Self-Portrait, November 1994–January 1995, 1994–95
Oil on linen
16×14 inches
Collection of Wheelock Whitney III, New York. Courtesy of CRG Gallery, New York

Portait of Paul, 1995
Oil on linen
16×14 inches
Collection of Ellyn and Saul Dennison, Bernardsville, N.J. Courtesy of CRG Gallery, New York

Cindy Sherman

Untitled, #250, 1992
Color photograph
50×75 inches

The Museum of Modern Art, New York. Gift of Werner and Elaine Dannheiser. Courtesy of the artist and Metro Pictures, New York

Susan Unterberg

Untitled from Father/Son series, 1990
Color Polaroids
24×20 inches each (two panels)
Collection of the New School for Social Research, New York. Courtesy of the artist

Untitled from Father/Son series, 1990
Color Polaroids
24×20 inches each (two panels)
Courtesy of the artist

Jeff Wall

The Giant, 1992
Cibachrome transparency, fluorescent light, display case, edition 1 AP
19½×23×4¾ inches
Courtesy of Marian Goodman Gallery, New York

Manabu Yamanaka

Gyahtei #6, 1995
Black-and-white photograph, edition of 9
68×31½ inches framed
Courtesy of Stefan Stux Gallery, New York

Gyahtei #7, 1995
Black-and-white photograph, edition of 9
68×31½ inches framed
Courtesy of Stefan Stux Gallery, New York

Richard Yarde

Coming and Going, 1996–97
Transparent and opaque watercolor
67½×180 inches
Courtesy of the artist

MOJO Hand, 1996–97
Transparent and opaque watercolor
76×148 inches
Courtesy of the artist

Lisa Yuskavage

"Manifest Destiny," 1998
Oil on linen
110×55 inches
Collection Museum of Contemporary Art, San Diego. Museum purchase, Contemporary Collectors Fund. Courtesy of Marianne Boesky Gallery, New York

Surrender, 1998
Oil on linen
36×36 inches
Courtesy of Marianne Boesky Gallery, New York

FILM AND VIDEO

Alan Berliner

Nobody's Business, 1996
16 mm film, 60:00 minutes
Courtesy of the artist

Arlene Bowman

Navajo Talking Pictures, 1986
16 mm film, 40:00 minutes
Courtesy of Women Make Movies, New York

Jean-François Brunet and Peter Friedman

The Life and Times of Life and Times, 1998
Betacam SP, 59:00 minutes
Courtesy of Emmanuel Laurent, producer, Films à Trois, Paris and Science TV Distribution, Canada

Liz Cane

Libido, 1989
16 mm film, 4:30 minutes
Courtesy of the artist

Alain Cavalier

Portraits, 1988–92
Video, 90:00 minutes
Courtesy of Douce Productions, Paris and Margaret Mead Film and Video Festival, American Museum of Natural History, New York

Susan Hadary Cohen and William Whiteford

Grace, 1991
Video, 58:00 minutes
Courtesy of UMAB Video Press, Baltimore

Sandi DuBowski

Tomboychik, 1994
8 mm video, 15:00 minutes
Courtesy of the artist and Video Data Bank, Chicago

Rebecca Feig

Bye-Bye Babushka, 1997
16 mm film, 80:00 minutes
Courtesy of the artist

Neil Goldberg

Untitled, 1999
Video, 2:30 minutes
Courtesy of the artist

Carol Halstead

Why?, 1994
16 mm film, 12:00 minutes
Courtesy of Moving Images Distribution, Inc., Vancouver, B.C.

Heddy Honigmann

O Amor Natural, 1997
35 mm film, 76:00 minutes
Courtesy of First Run Features, New York

Keiko Ibi

The Personals: Improvisations on Romance in the Golden Years, 1998
16 mm film, 37:00 minutes
Courtesy of the artist

Suzanne Lacy

Whisper, the Waves, the Wind, 1984
16 mm film documentation of performance on the beach in La Jolla, California, 28:00 minutes
Courtesy of the artist and Terra Nova Films, Inc., Chicago

Lisa Lewenz

A Letter Without Words, 1998
16 mm film, 62:00 minutes
Courtesy of the artist

Brad Lichtenstein

André's Lives, 1999
16 mm film, 55:00 minutes
Courtesy of Lumiere Productions, Inc., New York

Kiti Luostarinen

Gracious Curves, 1997
Video, 52:23 minutes
Courtesy of Epidem Oy, Helsinki and Margaret Mead Film and Video Festival, American Museum of Natural History, New York

Amanda Micheli

Just for the Ride: Bucking Convention, Cowgirl Style, 1996
16 mm film, 53:00 minutes
Courtesy of Runaway Productions, San Francisco

Tracey Moffatt

Night Cries, 1990
Film, 19:00 minutes
Courtesy of Women Make Movies, New York

Nigel Nobel

Close Harmony, 1981
16 mm film, 30:00 minutes
Courtesy of Filmakers Library, New York

Gail Noonan

Your Name in Cellulite, 1995
35 mm film, 6:00 minutes
Courtesy of Women Make Movies, New York

Older, Stronger, Wiser, 1990
16 mm film, 28:00 minutes
Produced by the Film Board of Canada. Courtesy of Indiana University Instructional Support Services, Bloomington

Jennifer Paige

Grandma's Hands, 1998
DV Cam, 27:57 minutes
Courtesy of the artist

Yvonne Rainer

Privilege, 1990
16 mm film, 103:00 minutes
Courtesy of Zeitgeist Films, New York

Joel Saxe

Yiddish Folksingers of Miami Beach, 1991
8 mm video and Super 8 film, 30:00 minutes
Courtesy of the artist

Cynthia Scott

Strangers in Good Company, 1990
35 mm film, 105:00 minutes
Courtesy of First Run Features, New York

Alice Stone

She Lives to Ride, 1994
16 mm film, 78:00 minutes (17:00 minutes, exhibition excerpt)
Courtesy of Women Make Movies, New York

Johnny Symons

Beauty Before Age, 1997
Betacam SP, 22:00 minutes
Courtesy of the artist

Agnes Varda

Sept Pieces, Cuisines, Salle de Bains [Seven Rooms, Kitchens, Bathrooms], 1984
35 mm film, 27:00 minutes
Courtesy of Ciné Tamaris, Paris

Lucy Winer and Karen Eaton

Golden Threads, 1999
Video, 56:00 minutes
Courtesy of Women Make Movies, New York

Jacob Young

Dancing Outlaw, 1992
Video, 30:00 minutes
Courtesy of the artist

TELEVISION PROGRAMS

All in the Family

Edith's Problem, 1971
Courtesy of Columbia TriStar Television

Cybill

When You're Hot, You're Hot, 1996
Courtesy of The Carsey-Werner Company

Daria

Write Where it Hurts, 1998
Courtesy of MTV Networks

Maude

Maude's Dilemma, Pt. 1, 1972
Maude's Dilemma, Pt. 2, 1972
Courtesy of Columbia TriStar Television

Sanford and Son

Happy Birthday, Pop, 1972
Courtesy of Columbia TriStar Television

The Simpsons

Lisa vs. Malibu Stacy, 1994 (excerpt)
Courtesy of Twentieth Century Fox Film Corporation

TELEVISION ADVERTISEMENTS

IBM

French Guys, 1994
Courtesy of IBM and Ogilvy & Mather, New York

McDonald's

The New Kid, 1987
Courtesy of McDonald's Corporation

Nike

Hijack Footwear, 1984
Courtesy of Nike, Inc. and Wieden & Kennedy, Portland

Volvo

Sauna, 1973
Courtesy of Volvo Cars of North America, Inc. and Messner, Vetere, Berger, McNamee, Schmetterer/Euro RSCG, New York

Wendy's

Fluffy Bun, 1983
Courtesy of Wendy's International

INTERACTIVE PROJECTS THROUGH THE VISUAL KNOWLEDGE PROGRAM (VKP)

Lynne Yamamoto with Pam Simon, Dara Winkler, and Kathryn McCarthy

The Struggle for Civil Rights: An Intergenerational Fable, 1998-98
American Social History Project class, IAT
Video and photographs

Juan Jose Robles with Marijke Hecht and Meryl Meisler

Senescence of $Ca_{10}(PO_4)_6(OH)_2$, 1998–99
Chemistry class, ICE
Mixed media installation

Todd Ayoung with Diane Varano

Time Machine, 1998–99
Environmental Studies class, IAT
Mixed media installation

OTHER PROJECTS

Time Slips
Installation of photographs and handmade books relating to an interactive, intergenerational storytelling project with people with Alzheimer's
Ten photographs, 20×24 inches each unframed
Two books, 16×42×10 inches each
Project Director: Anne Davis Basting
Project Associate: Nichole Griffith
Photographer: Dick Blau
Book Artist: Beth Thielen
Web Designer: Chad Anderson
Videographer/Sound Designer: Xavier LePlae

PERFORMANCES

Tim Erikson

Singer/Musician

Kim Irwin and Max Below Toledo-Paris

On My Honor I Will Do My Best
Performance

J Mandle Performance

When
Broadway window performances

Helen Schneyer

Singer/Musician

Artists' Statements*

**The statements only represent a portion of those artists included in the exhibition.*

Todd Ayoung (40)

In my case, with age comes more responsibility to my family. Having children (two) takes up a lot of time, which means I do not have much time for "art," in the traditional studio sense. Having children "ages" one, "youth" is something that is transferred to your children. When I was younger it was easier to isolate the art practice from the larger goings on in the world—idealism and singularity was my god! Being the age I am now, it is harder to separate the complexities of everyday life and this little world called art.

Anne Davis Basting (33)

At a very basic level, this work, which I see as large scale, performative public art, stems from a yearning to connect with the darkest, scariest place in the life course. It's a place where we, as we know ourselves now (and that we so easily trick ourselves into believing is immortal) evaporate, leaving behind the dry shell of an often (cruelly) intact body. Is there a person there? Are "we" so separate from "them"—these people with dementia?

On a personal level, I now see all my work (creative and scholarly) as an incessant search for my grandmother's voice; for the untold stories that were stolen by the stroke that deadened her tongue for the last five years of her life. In photos, I see myself in her cheekbones, her chin, her posture. Perhaps because of those similarities, she was the only one I let tell me what to do. I didn't always do it of course . . . But there is something so comforting about confident direction, whether you follow it or not. It's embarrassingly simple really. I miss her. I miss the force of her observations on life, sometimes wildly off mark, sometimes dead on.

Alan Berliner (42)

Like most artists, each work I make places me at the threshold of becoming. Takes me to the crossroads of who I was, who I am and who I imagine I want to be. To the boundaries of my own inner contradictions.

In order to make *Nobody's Business,* an intimate portrait of my eighty year old father, Oscar, I had to be just vulnerable enough to contemplate transforming the personal into the public, yet just courageous enough to believe it was for a good reason. Just dumb enough to think I could do it, but then just smart enough to pull it off. And, as in the making of any work of art that focuses life through the prism of time, just young enough and/but just old enough . . .

Just young enough not to know any better. Just old enough to really care. Just young enough to not ask for anybody's permission. Just old enough to know if I didn't do it now, I might never have another chance. Young enough to rush in recklessly. Old enough to take my time leaving. Young enough to ask ten thousand questions. Old enough to let a few go unanswered. Young enough to have a quick left jab. Old enough to know when to take a punch. Young enough to hate losing. Old enough to let him win. (Some of the time, anyway.) Young enough to still be his dutiful son. Too old to still call him Daddy. Young enough to think I can keep him from growing old. Old enough to know better. Young enough to be exasperated, even angry. Old enough to show my love. Young and stubborn. Older and even more stubborn.

Chakaia Booker

I Did Not Think About Age Early.

During childhood I was told I would "never amount to anything" and my focus was "don't quit—don't quit." Age has helped me to think less about quitting when it comes to personal goals and aspirations about life's unfolding into daily repetitive stationary scenarios.

Age gave me voice and dialogue to communicate my inner thoughts individually, collectively, and universally. My work is a way of exposing and understanding my internal feelings. The work is a vehicle to communicate when I was taught early not to communicate. By producing the work I can finally release myself of some of the emotional entanglements and make others aware of what has been and is happening.

Age has helped me to see the impotence of ingrained energy. This awakening makes it necessary to flush out those impurities invading cultural, social, and economic life. Emerging new energy allows me to respond in a guerrilla state of deliverance consistent with a holistic and humanistic view of humanity. These impulses arrive through empowerment and acknowledgment of past and present achievements on a personal and collective level. The emerging awareness expressed through my work is a lifetime process. Hopefully, I eliminate cultural attitudes and myths that people hold about women and aging.

How Old Would You Like Me to Be?

As a woman of color from the lower class it feels like I was born old—outdated. Over-burdened intellectually but underused—siphoned, but rarely, if ever, solicited. Born depreciated in value, depreciated even more through lack of care. Deterioration of the physical body beginning at birth—if not directly started before birth—"early" loss of hair, teeth, general health, and abuse shown in the indifference to regular care. All are symbolic reflections seen in my art.

Nancy Burson (51)

Since my hair turned gray, I prefer to work in color.

Bruce Cannon (39)

I find that as I age I am rapidly losing my sense of invincibility, and consequently find myself approaching the subject of mortality with a great deal more difficulty, if not pain. I still cling to the belief that quality of life is determined by the act of dying, and for that reason mortality must be cherished. Yet in recent years this polemic has begun to feel a bit glib, and I have come to face the possibility that I may well abandon it in the face of my own ongoing struggle with the meaning of my life and eventual death. For what new philosophy, I don't yet know...

Harriet Casdin-Silver (74)

I am finally able to employ
All the advice I give my students
Free up inside gamble on yourself dare to fail
Loose loose cut the noose
Freedom is the key to originality
At 70 + 4 I set my own standards
I need no experts
I am the expert

Of course I am still a young old
A healthy old and a well-fed old
There are young old and mid old and old old
There are healthy old and sick old
Rich old and poor old

Much territory and big issues to explore in the 21st century
I have a lot to do the next one-third of my life

Sandi DuBowski (28)

Age can sweeten and open or it can shut people down. I was twenty-two when my grandmother and I did *Tomboychik*. I hope the sweetness of those moments stay with me.

Jacqueline Hayden (49)

I read recently that if you had a baby late in your reproductive life (I had one at forty-three) you have the genetic make up to live to be one hundred years old. I pause to consider the next fifty years. As an aging woman, I am particularly impressed by how invisible we are in our cultural lexicon except as grandmothers, witches and hags. I hope to contribute an alternative vision.

J Mandle Performance (3)

How do we perceive getting older? How closely do we notice time passing? When are we conscious of a change? In our world of rapid and constant change, when do we stop and ask ourselves these questions? All three of these topics are inextricably bound together and have a profound effect on the way we perceive ourselves. Likewise, our sense of self controls our capacity to experience the process of aging, time, and change.

In the context of busy metropolitan New York, the storefront window performance *When* will offer a visual alternative to our anxious environment by identifying a basic principle of time: the perception of change. The performance structure is based on a sundial instrument and marks how our contemporary society has moved away from intimacy with natural fluctuations to measured time.

Time can be understood as a subjective experience and as a function of our consciousness. How time is perceived will define the perceiver. The performance *When* intends to draw attention to the audience member's perception of aging by exposing one's temporal expectations of the environment. What is one's sense of identity in the face of this experience? Can one perceive discontinuity in change?

Yoshiko Kanai (43)

I came to feel that as I went through the process of constructing my work, I also assembled or defined my own consciousness. When I was a young woman, I couldn't make my face with my body. I was afraid that audiences would know that my work came from my emotional experiences. I wondered how I looked to society. Did my audience see me as a good daughter, a good wife, a good teacher, or a troubled woman? My father had a respected position as a professor of child psychology. I was afraid my work would jeopardize his position because my work is controversial in Japan. As I became older and by living in the U.S., I have gotten more confidence as an artist. Even though I use my body in my work, the audience and I can share our lives through my work, if my work reveals emotional reality.

Suzanne Lacy (53)

I don't notice the effect of age on my work yet, except that I am more knowledgeable about social systems and potential points of intervention, public strategies and how to operate on larger scales. These are probably more attributable to increased experience, which comes with age.

However, I have always been sensitive to issues of aging. I began making performances on the theme in the mid-seventies. A good deal of my work was about the physical body, the mind's conversations with that body, the vulnerability of the body, and its inevitable deterioration—through aging, at the very least, and possibly through illness as well. The attraction to aging as subject was part curiosity about a physical body whose processes were not in one's control, and part awareness of how perceptions of the aged often resulted in prejudice and oppression. My most well-known work has taken a social justice direction that appears, and is, meant to be about changing attitudes, but the personal subtext of this work is a continuing interest I have in what aging and dissolution mean to consciousness encased in flesh.

Micah Lexier (38)

My age (and the ages of the individuals who are the subjects in my work) is a central and guiding force in most of my work and has been made explicit through the use of titles including:

Autobiography (Evelyn age 67), 1992

A Portrait of the Artist as a Slide (divided proportionally between life lived and life to come, based on a life expectancy of 75 years), 1994

A work of art in the form of a quantity of coins equal to the number of months of the statistical life expectancy of a child born January 6, 1995, 1995

A portrait of the Watson Family as a bronze casting of a coil of rope the length of which in inches is the cumulative statistical life expectancy in years of the 7 individual family members with a knot marking the moment when this was made, 1995

A Minute of My Time (January 5, 1996 22:50–22:51), 1996

Self-portrait as a thin red line dividing a piece of paper proportionally between an area representing life lived and an area representing life to come, based on statistical life expectancy, 1997

Brad Lichtenstein (30)

My age was crucial in my work for a simple reason. The gulf of time between André and I was sobering. It forced me to accept his right to own his attitude towards the past. When it comes to the Holocaust, there is a lot of competition among Jews, historians, institutions, and current morality to own Survivor's pasts. André was thirty—my age—when he bribed Nazis. He was my age when his parents were murdered. His choice to repress his Holocaust experience is something that I struggled to understand. I explored it beyond what he would have preferred for the sake of the film. I urged his children to pursue their desire to know more about his past. But, in the end, the full scope of André's life (he's on his way to 91) reveals some unmovable truth about all of us. We are the sole authors of our lives, and ultimately it is our responsibility alone to come to terms with the decisions we make.

Jennifer Paige (42)

My age (forty-two) has made a tremendous difference in my work because I did not get involved in filmmaking until I was in my thirties. I had just gotten divorced and had two small children and decided to return to school. It was then that I discovered my desire to make films and have been productive ever since.

I think my experience as a single parent/adult student gave me an affinity for the subject matter of my film—grandparents who raise their grandchildren. It takes a tremendous commitment to do a good job parenting and a lot of self-sacrifice, while at the same time taking good enough care of yourself so you can do the job right. Grandparents who take on the parenting face even more challenges and the job they do is astonishing.

Yvonne Rainer (64)

I turned to film as my dancer's body aged. My films have in part followed the concerns of my age and aging. At the risk of being reductive you might say my concerns aged as my focus moved from sexual conflict in the early 70s to social constructs in the 80s and 90s.

Jeffrey Saldinger (52)

As time goes by, my engagement with my work becomes more important to me. I continue to refine the ways I've developed to use time well.

Joel Saxe (41)

I was a kid in the 1960s and had parents in the arts—my mother was a ballet and modern dancer and my father was in the theater—who came of age in the 1930s. My father was fifty when I was born and had been a lefty workers' theatre activist. Though we live with tremendous anti-communism in this country, I grew up seeing an old man who was loving and gentle and artistic and just wanted to make the world a place where all people had economic and social justice. My mother wasn't quite as political, but she too was quite progressive and outspoken for peoples' rights. When we went to peace rallies, a group of old radicals from Miami Beach were always there, a backbone of the movement. My grandfather lived in an old hotel a block from the ocean where I visited quite often. The memories of that scene stayed with me and compelled a documentary project seeking to record what was once a thriving Yiddish medina. Voz iz gevan, iz gevan. What used to be is what used to be. I don't want to be nostalgic here, but it's about understanding where we came from, what to hold onto, and maybe what's been lost in the post-modern rush.

Helen Schneyer (78)

Age has not basically changed my work, except to intensify my feeling for traditional American folk music and how singing it allows me to speak musically what is more difficult for me to say in spoken words. Age has also made clear how grateful I am for the gift of my voice and how much satisfaction in living comes from singing whether it is in concert or when I do my daily work at the piano at the unspeakable time of 6 a.m.

Cindy Sherman (44)

I can see myself aging in the work itself.

Johnny Symons (33)

As a thirty-three-year-old gay male, I feel I am on the fence between the younger and middle-aged gay communities. Having directed an HIV-prevention program for young gay men, I have witnessed the anger and fear youth have towards older men, and the resentment, envy, and dismissal which older men often feel towards the younger generation. I created Beauty Before Age to explore this divide and to encourage people all along the spectrum of aging to look for ways to bridge their differences. My age puts me in a privileged position of being able to view both worlds and to explore my own misgivings and hopes about growing older.

Max Below Toledo-Paris (50) + Kim Irwin (52)

Now that we are over-fifty adults . . .

WE ARE NOT DEAD YET
We still try to be IDEAL CITIZENS
We recognize and celebrate each other and our MIDDLE CLASS American values and beliefs
We detect, reveal and exploit CONTRADICTIONS in our daily lives
We pass on unrelenting stereotypes to future generations
We are INCLUSIVE of those who make us HAPPY
We are playful with our desires and curiosities
We keep ourselves VISUALLY AND POETICALLY EXCITED about who we are and what we are doing
WE ARE GOING FOR BROKE
We are founding directors of ELDER SEX
We are open, HONEST and sex-driven
We know the grass isn't GREENER
We realize you only live once
We love to FANTASIZE and be irreverent
WE ARE AN OVERNIGHT SUCCESS DAILY
We regress as needed
We re-enact our youth when inappropriate
We have uncontrollable DESIRES
We are aging cultural icons whose only connection to the meaning of life is Tupperware
We love FAMILY VALUES
We acknowledge our genius every minute
We love aesthetics when they are convenient
We worship vibration and having FUNDAMENTAL FUN
WE ARE FASHION conscious with a conscience
WE ARE SUBMISSIVE TO EVERYTHING WHENEVER POSSIBLE
We try not to get drunk in public
WE ARE IN LOVE
We are ready to surrender at any moment
WE ARE FOOLISH
We renounce and enjoy
We are amazed at ourselves
We think in pictures not words
We surrender to wild, UNDISCIPLINED LAUGHTER
We are obsessed by taste and smell
We are reclaiming our authentic selves
We invent new possibilities of pleasure
WE DRESS UP

Susan Unterberg (57)

Age has given me perspective. It has allowed me to look deep within myself. When photographing family relationships, I can identify with both parent and child.

Age has allowed me to be myself. I no longer feel that I must please. I'm at a time in my life when everything is coming together. All the struggles in my past surprisingly prepared me for the present. I'm seasoned. The work continues to get richer and I seem to grow stronger year by year!

Manabu Yamanaka (39)

I was often asked to provide an explanation of the title of my photographs, *Gyahtei*, but I would prefer to refrain from attempting to explain the meaning of this Buddhist term as I feel that to do so would in some way distract the viewer from the uniqueness of my work. I am not an expert on Buddhist theology and my choice for a title is done merely on personal interpretation after the fact. I take photographs relying on instinct and the five senses. Viewers are asked to consider *Gyahte*i as a kind of magical word like Aladdin's "Open Sesame" wherein each person can interpret for himself or herself what the title means. By not explaining, my work will take on a kind of life of its own, step into the hearts of each of the viewers and take on its own personality. Of course, I have my own thoughts on it as well . . .

Richard Yarde (59)

In 1991, at the age of fifty-one, I nearly died from kidney failure. I was physically and spiritually broken after my hospitalization. Soon after being released from the hospital, I went on dialysis, which has burdened my wife, Susan, and me to the breaking point. I decided to explore alternative approaches to healing.

I experimented with chiropractic rehabilitation and massage. I also attended religious services conducted by Father Ralph DeOrio, a Catholic priest with a healing ministry and worked with a Jungian therapist for two years.

After more than a year of slow, painful rehabilitation, I returned to the studio. My illness had been a shattering experience but it had also jolted me into the present and inspired dramatic changes in the content of my painting.

The painting allowed me to explore the negative and positive aspects of transformation from fragmentation to wholeness. Fragility and contradiction became the central issues of my work.

I wanted to create of a body of work based on faith. Recently I have had a kidney transplant that has brought a renewed level of energy back into my life: A rebirth. I feel that the world as I have come to know it is very mysterious and I would like to make work that parallels that mystery in some way.

Lisa Yuskavage (39)

The older I get the more seriously people take what I say, so I have no comment.

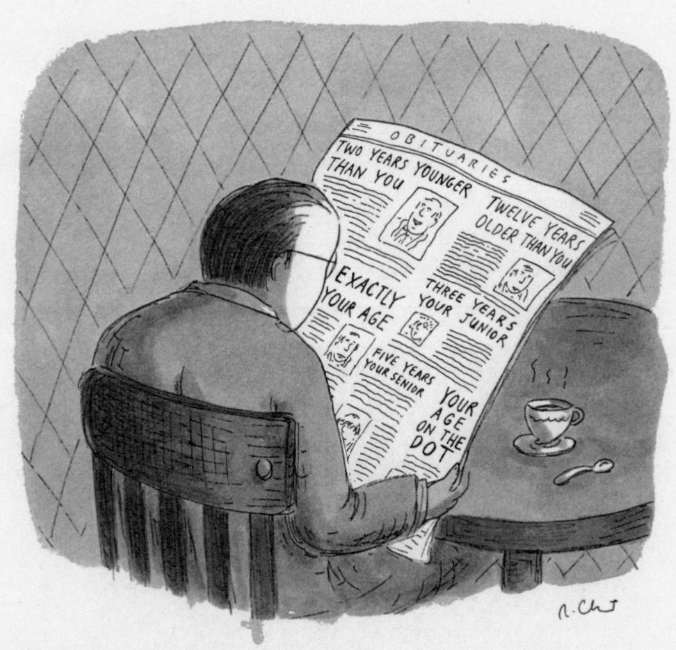

Roz Chast. ©The New Yorker Collection 1998 Roz Chast from cartoonbank.com. All Rights Reserved.

Selected Bibliography: Partial, Unfinished, and Only Slightly Biased

Achenbaum, W. A. *Crossing Frontiers: Gerontology Emerges as a Science*. New York: Cambridge University Press, 1995.

_____. *Old Age in the New Land: The American Experience Since 1790*. Baltimore: Johns Hopkins University Press, 1978.

_____. *Shades of Gray: Old Age, American Values, and Federal Policies Since 1920*. Boston: Little, Brown, 1983.

Achenbaum, W.A. and Vern L. Bengston. *The Changing Contract Across Generations*. New York: Adline de Gruyter, 1993.

Achenbaum, W.A., Thomas R. Cole, Patricia L. Jakobi, and Robert Kastenbaum, eds. *Voices and Visions of Aging: Toward a Critical Gerontology*. New York: Springer, 1993.

Allen, Jessie and Alan Pifer, eds. *Women on the Front Lines: Meeting the Challenge of an Aging America*. Washington D.C.: Urban Institute Press, 1993.

Angel, R.J. and J.L. Angel. *Who Will Care For Us? Aging and Long-Term Care in Multicultural America*. New York: New York University Press, 1997.

Applewhite, S.R., ed. *Hispanic Elderly in Transition*. New York: Greenwood Press, 1988.

Arber, Sara and Maria Evandrou, eds. *Ageing, Independence, and the Life Course*. London: Jessica Kingsley in association with the British Society of Gerontology, 1993.

Arber, Sara and Jay Ginn. *Gender and Later Life: A Sociological Analysis of Resources and Contraints*. Newbury Park, Cal.: Sage Publications, 1991.

_____, eds. *Connecting Gender and Ageing: A Sociological Approach*. Philadelphia: Open University Press, 1995.

Ariès, Philippe. *Centuries of Childhood*. New York: Vintage Books, 1965.

Asher, Mary and Neil Postman. *The Disappearance of Childhood*. New York: Vintage Books, 1994.

Banner, Lois W. *In Full Flower: Aging Women, Power, and Sexuality: A History*. New York: Knopf, 1992.

Barresi, C.M. and D.E. Gelfand, eds. *Ethnic Dimensions of Aging*. New York: Springer, 1987.

Bartz, Walter. *Dare to Be 100*. New York: Simon and Schuster, 1995.

Basting, Anne Davis. *The Stages of Age: Performing Age in Contemporary American Culture*. Ann Arbor: University of Michigan Press, 1998.

Beck, Kristin and Lauren Dockett. *Facing 30: Women Talk About Constructing a Real Life and Other Scary Rites of Passage*. Oakland, Cal.: New Harbinger Publications, Inc., 1998.

Becker, Ernest. *The Denial of Death*. New York: Free Press, 1973.

Birren, James E., Gary M. Kenyon, and Johannes J. F. Schroots, eds. *Metaphors of Aging in Science and the Humanities*. New York: Springer, 1991.

Birren, James E. and Linda Feldman. *Where to Go from Here: Discovering Your Own Life's Wisdom in Your Second Fifty*. New York: Simon and Schuster, 1997.

Bliss, Jeff and Susan Perlstein. *Generating Community: Intergenerational programs through the Expressive Arts*. Brooklyn, N.Y.: Elders Share the Arts, 1994.

Booth, Wayne C., ed. *The Art of Growing Older: Writers on Living and Aging*. Chicago: The University of Chicago Press, 1992.

Boyle, Joan M. and James E. Morriss. *The Mirror of Time: Images of Aging and Dying*. Westport, Conn.: Greenwood Press, 1987.

Brehony, Kathleen A. *Awakening at Midlife: Realizing Your Potential for Growth and Change*. New York: Riverhead Books, 1996.

Brubaker, T.H., ed. *Family Relationships in Later Life*. Newbury Park, Cal.: Sage Publications, 1990.

Bynum, Caroline Walker. *The Resurrection of the Body in Western Christianity, 200–1326*. New York: Columbia University Press, 1995.

Bytheway, Bill. *Ageism*. Buckingham: Open University Press, 1995.

Callahan, Joan, ed. *Menopause: A Midlife Passage*. Bloomington: Indiana University Press, 1993.

Carter, Jimmy. *The Virtues of Aging*. New York: The Library of Contemporary Thought, 1998.

Cash, Thomas. "The Psychology of Physical Appearance: Aesthetics, Attributes, and Images," in *Body Images: Development, Deviance, and Change*. Edited by T.F. Cash and T. Pruzinsky. New York: Guilford Press, 1990.

Cassata, Dr. Mary. *Television Looks at Aging*. New York: Television Information Office, 1985.

Chapkis, Wendy. *Beauty Secrets: Women and the Politics of Appearance*. Boston: South End, 1986.

Charmaz, Kathy and Jaber F. Gubrium. *Aging, Self and Community: A Collection of Readings*. Greenwich, Conn.: JAI Press, 1992.

Chudacoff, Howard P. *How Old Are You? Age Consciousness in American Culture*. Princeton, N.J.: Princeton University Press, 1989.

Cohen, Joan Z., Karen Levin Coburn, and Joan Pearlman. *Hitting Our Stride: Good News About Women in Their Middle Years*. New York: Delacorte Press, 1980.

Cohen, Lawrence. *No Aging in India: Alzheimer's, the Bad Family, and Other Modern Things*. Berkeley: University of California Press, 1998.

Cole, Ellen, Nancy D. Davis, and Esther D. Rothblum, eds. *Faces of Women and Aging*. New York: Haworth Press, 1993.

Cole, Thomas R. *The Journey of Life: A Cultural History of Aging in America*. New York: Cambridge University Press, 1992.

Cole, Thomas R., et al., eds. *Voices and Visions of Aging: Toward a Critical Gerontology*. New York: Springer Publishing Company, 1993.

Cole, Thomas R. and Sally A. Gadow. *What Does It Mean to Grow Old? Reflections from the Humanities.* Durham, N.C.: Duke University Press, 1986.

Cole, Thomas R., Robert Kastenbaum, and David D. Van Tassel, eds. *Handbook on the Humanities and Aging.* New York: Springer, 1992.

Cole, Thomas R. and Mary G. Winkler. *The Oxford Book of Aging.* New York: Oxford University Press, 1994.

Cole, William, ed. *When You Consider the Alternative: Enlightening and Amusing Words on Age and Aging.* New York: St. Martin's Press, 1996.

Coney, Sandra. *The Menopause Industry: How the Medical Establishment Exploits Women.* Alameda, Cal.: Hunter House, 1994.

Cornell, Virginia. *The Latest Wrinkle: And Other Signs of Aging.* Carpinteria, Cal.: Manifest Publications, 1996.

Coupland, Justine, Nikolas Coupland, and Howard Giles. *Language, Society and the Elderly: Discourse, Identity and Ageing.* Oxford: Blackwell, 1991.

Covey, Herbert C. *Images of Older People in Western Art and Society.* New York: Praeger, 1991.

de Beauvoir, Simone. *The Coming of Age.* Translated by Patrick O'Brian. 1970. Reprint. New York: Putnam, 1972.

_____. *Old Age.* Translated by Patrick O'Brian. London: Weidenfeld and Nicolson, 1972.

_____. *The Second Sex.* Translated and edited by H. M. Parshley. 1949. Reprint. New York: Knopf, 1953.

de Luce, Judith and Thomas M. Falkner, eds. *Old Age in Greek and Latin Literature.* New York: State University of New York Press, 1989.

Dowling, Colette. *Red Hot Mamas: Coming Into Our Own at Fifty.* New York: Bantam Books, 1996.

Erikson, Erik, ed. *Adulthood.* New York: Norton, 1978.

Erikson, Erik, Joan Erikson, and Helen Kivnick. *Vital Involvement in Old Age.* New York: Norton, 1986.

Erikson, Erik and Neil Smelser. *Themes of Work and Love in Adulthood.* Cambridge, Mass.: Harvard University Press, 1980.

Estes, Carroll L., *The Long Term Care Crisis: Elders Trapped in the No-Care Zone.* Newbury Park, Cal.: Sage Publications, 1993.

Estes, Carroll L. and Meredith Minkler. *Critical Gerontology: Perspectives from Political and Moral Exonomy.* Amityville, N.Y.: Baywood Publishing Co., 1999.

Evandrou, Maria, ed. *Babyboomers: Ageing in the 21st Century.* London: Age Concern England, 1997.

Facio, Elisa. *Understanding Older Chicanos: Sociological and Public Policy Perspectives.* Thousand Oaks, Cal.: Sage Publications, 1991.

Falk, Ursula A. and Gerhard Falk. *Ageism, the Aged, and Aging in America: On Being Old in an Alienated Society.* Springfield, Ill.: C.C. Thomas Publisher, 1997.

Featherstone, Mike and Mike Hepworth. *Surviving Middle Age.* Oxford: B. Blackwell, 1982.

Featherstone, Mike and Andrew Wernick. *Images of Aging: Cultural Representation of Later Life.* New York: Routledge, 1995.

Fraser, Kennedy. *Ornament and Silence: Essays on Women's Lives.* New York: Alfred A. Knopf, 1996.

Freeman, Joseph T. *Aging: Its History and Literature.* New York: Human Sciences Press, 1979.

Friedan, Betty. *The Fountain of Age.* New York: Simon and Schuster, 1993.

Furman, Frida Kemer. *Facing the Mirror: Older Women and Beauty Shop Culture.* New York: Routledge, 1997.

Garcia, A. and M. Sotomayor, eds. *Elderly Latinos.* Washington D.C.: National Hispanic Council on Aging, 1993.

Gatens, Moira. *Imaginary Bodies: Ethics, Power, and Corporeality.* London: Routledge, 1995.

Gilman, Sander L. *Making the Body Beautiful: A Cultural History of Aesthetic Surgery.* Princeton, N.J.: Princeton University Press, 1999.

Greer, Germaine. *The Change.* London: Hamish Hamilton, 1991.

Grosz, Elizabeth. *Space, Time, and Perversion. Essays on the Politics of Bodies.* London: Routledge, 1995.

Gubrium, Jaber F. *Time, Roles and Self in Old Age.* New York: Human Sciences Press, 1976.

Gullette, Margaret Morganroth. *Declining to Decline: Cultural Combat and the Politics of the Midlife.* Charlottesville: University Press of Virginia, 1997.

_____. *Safe at Last in the Middle Years: The Invention of the Midlife Progress Novel.* Berkeley: University of California Press, 1989.

Haiken, Elizabeth. *Venus Envy: A History of Cosmetic Surgery.* Baltimore: The Johns Hopkins University Press, 1997.

Hammond, Doris B. *My Parents Never Had Sex: Myths and Facts of Sexual Aging.* Buffalo, N.Y.: Prometheus Books, 1987.

Hayflick, Leonard. *How and Why We Age.* New York: Ballantine Books, 1994.

Hazan, Haim. *Old Age: Constructions and Deconstructions.* Cambridge: Cambridge University Press, 1994.

Heilbrun, Carolyn G. *The Last Gift of Time: Life Beyond Sixty.* New York: The Dial Press, 1997.

Hendricks, Jon and Davis Hendricks. *Dimensions of Aging: Readings.* Cambridge, Mass.: Winthrop Publishers, 1979.

Hockey, Jenny and Allison James. *Growing Up and Growing Old: Ageing and Dependency in the Life Course.* London: Sage Publications, 1993.

Holbrook, Nikki J., George R. Martin, and Richard A. Lockshin. *Cellular Aging and Cell Death.* New York: Wiley-Liss, 1996.

Holmes, Ellen Rhoads. *Other Cultures, Elder Years.* Thousand Oaks, Cal.: Sage Publications, 1995.

Hooper, John and Patricia Jalland, eds. *Women From Birth to Death: The Female Life Cycle in Britain 1830–1914.* Atlantic Highlands, N.J.: Humanitites Press, 1986.

Hunter, Ski and Martin Sundel. *Midlife Myths: Issues, Findings, and Practice Implications.* Newbury Park, Cal.: Sage Publications, 1989.

Isay, David and Harvey Wang. *Holding On: Dreamers, Visionaries, Eccentrics, and Other American Heroes.* New York: W.W. Norton and Company, 1996.

Jackson, J.S., et al., eds. *Aging in Black America.* Newbury Park, Cal.: Sage Publications, 1993.

Kahn, PhD., Robert L. and John Wallis Rowe, M.D. *Successful*

Aging. New York: Pantheon Books, 1998.

Katz, Stephen. *Disciplining Old Age: The Formation of Gerontological Knowledge*. Charlottesville: University Press of Virginia, 1996.

Kausler, Barry C. and Donald H. Kausler. *The Graying of America: An Encyclopedia of Aging, Health, Mind, and Behavior*. Urbana: University of Illinois Press, 1996.

Keigher, Sharon. *Housing Risks and Homelessness Among the Urban Elderly*. New York: Haworth Press, 1991.

Keith, Jeanie, et al., eds. *The Aging Experience*. Thousand Oaks, Cal.: Sage Publications, 1994.

Kertzer, David I. and Peter Laslett. *Aging in the Past: Demography, Society, and Old Age*. Berkeley: University of California Press, 1995.

Kitano, Harry H.L. *Generations and Identity: The Japanese American*. Needham Heights, Mass.: Ginn Press, 1993.

Labouvie-Vief, Gisela. "Psychological Transformations and Late-Life Creativity," in *Bulletin: The University of Michigan Museums of Art and Archaeology XI, 1994–96*. Ann Arbor: The Kelsey Museum of Archaeology, University of Michigan, 1996.

Laslett, Peter. *A Fresh Map of Life: The Emergence of the Third Age*. Cambridge, Mass.: Harvard University Press, 1991.

Ledoux, Denis. *Turning Memories Into Memoirs: A Handbook for Writing Life Stories*. Lisbon Falls, Me.: Soleil Press, 1993.

Levin, Jack. *Ageism: Prejudice and Discrimination Against the Elderly*. Belmont, Cal.: Wadsworth Publishing, 1980.

Levinson, Daniel. *The Seasons of a Man's Life*. New York: Knopf, 1978.

Levinson, Daniel and Judy D. Levinson. *The Seasons of a Woman's Life*. New York: Knopf, 1996.

Love, Dr. Susan with Karen Lindsey. *Dr. Susan Love's Hormone Book: Making Informed Choices About Menopause*. New York: Random House, 1997.

Macdonald, Barbara and Cynthia Rich. *Look Me in the Eye: Old Women, Aging and Ageism*. San Francisco: Spinsters Book Company, 1983.

Markides, Kyriakos and Manuel Miranda. *Minorities, Aging and Health*. Thousand Oaks, Cal.: Sage Publications, 1997.

McLerran, Jennifer. *Old Age in Myth and Symbol: A Cultural Dictionary*. New York: Greenwood Press, 1991.

Medina, John. *The Clock of Ages: Why We Age – How We Age – Winding Back the Clock*. Cambridge: Cambridge University Press, 1996.

Melamed, Elissa. *Mirror, Mirror: The Terror of Not Being Young*. New York: Linden, 1983.

Mellencamp, Patricia. *High Anxiety: Catastrophe, Scandal, Age and Comedy*. Bloomington: Indiana University Press, 1992.

Meyers, Diana Tietjens. *Subjection and Subjectivity: Psychoanalytic Feminism and Moral Philosophy*. London: Routledge, 1994.

Miller, Henry. *On Turning Eighty*. Santa Barbara, Cal.: Capra Press, 1972.

Minois, Georges. *History of Old Age: From Antiquity to the Renaissance*. Translated by Sarah Hanbury Tenison. Chicago: University of Chicago Press, 1989.

Moody, Harry R. *Abundance of Life: Human Development Policies for an Aging Society*. New York: Columbia University Press, 1988.

National Resource Center on Minority Aging Populations. *Ethnicity and Aging: Mental Health Issues*. San Diego, Cal.: National Resource Center on Minority Aging Populations, University Center on Aging, San Diego State University, 1990.

Neugarten, Dail A., ed. *The Meanings of Age: Selected Papers of Bernice L. Neugarten*. Chicago: The University of Chicago Press, 1996.

Norman, Alison. *Aspects of Ageism: A Discussion Paper*. London: Centre for Policy on Ageing, London, 1987.

Parrot, T. and J. Steckenrider, eds. *New Directions in Old Age Policy*. New York: State University of New York Press, 1997.

Peterson, Peter G. *Gray Dawn: How the Coming Age Wave Will Tranform America—And the World*. New York: Random House, 1999.

Pogrebin, Letty Cottin. *Getting Over Getting Older: An Intimate Journey*. Boston: Little, Brown, 1996.

Porter, Laurel, et al. *Aging in Literature*. Troy, Mich.: International Book Publishers, 1984.

Posner, Richard A. *Aging and Old Age*. Chicago: The University of Chicago Press, 1995.

Premo, Terri L. *Winter Friends: Women Growing Old in the New Repulic, 1785–1835*. Urbana: University of Illinois Press, 1990.

Rasmussen, Susan J. *The Poetics and Politics of Tuareg Aging: Life Course and Personal Destiny in Niger*. DeKalb: Northern Illinois University Press, 1997.

Rosenthal, Evelyn R., ed. *Women, Aging and Ageism*. New York: Harrington Park Press, 1990.

Rosenthal, Sylvia. *Cosmetic Surgery: A Consumer's Guide*. Philadelphia: J.B. Lippincott, 1977.

Rossen, Janice and Anne Wyatt-Brown, eds. *Aging and Gender in Literature: Studies in Creativity*. Charlottesville: University Press of Virginia, 1993.

Rossi, Alice S. "Sex and Gender in an Aging Society." *Daedalus* 115 (Winter 1986): 141–69.

Schwartz, Murray M. and Kathleen Woodward, eds. *Memory and Desire: Aging, Literature, Psychoanalysis*. Bloomington: Indiana University Press, 1986.

Schweitzer, Marjorie M. *Anthropology of Aging: A Partially Annotated Bibiliography*. New York: Greenwood Press, 1991.

Shedletsky, Stuart. *Still Working: Underknown Artists of Age in America*. New York: Parsons School of Design, in association with University of Washington Press, Seattle, 1994.

Sheehy, Gail. *The Silent Passage: Menopause*. New York: Random House, 1992.

_____. *Understanding Men's Passages: Discovering the New Map of Men's Lives*. New York: Random House, 1998.

Shuldiner, David Phillip. *Folklore, Culture and Aging: A Research Guide*. Westport, Conn.: Greenwood Press, 1997.

Shweder, Richard A., ed. *Welcome to Middle Age! (and Other Cultural Fictions)*. Chicago: University of Chicago Press, 1998.

Smith, Jean Louise. *Portraits of Aging*. Winona, Minn.: St. Mary's Press, 1972.

Sokolovsky, Jay, ed. *The Cultural Context of Aging*. New York: Bregin and Garvey, 1990.

____. *Growing Old in Different Societies: Cross-Cultural Perspectives.* Littleton, Mass.: Copley Publishing Group, 1987.

Stanek, Lou Willett. *Writing Your Life: Putting Your Past on Paper.* New York: Avon Books, 1996.

Strauss, Peter J., et al. *Aging and the Law.* Chicago: Commerce Clearing House, 1990.

Talley, James. *Aging: The Process, The Perception*. Exhibition catalogue. Jamestown, N.Y.: Forum Gallery, Jamestown Community College, 1990.

Terkel, Studs. *Coming of Age: The Story of Our Century By Those Who've Lived It*. New York: The New Press, 1995.

Vincent, John A. *Inequality and Old Age*. New York: St. Martin's Press, 1995.

Virilio, Paul. *Aesthetics of Disappearance*. Translated by Philip Beitchman. New York: Semiotext(e), 1991.

von Dorotka Bagnell, Prisca and Patricia Spencer Soper, eds. *Perceptions of Aging in Literature: A Cross-Cultural Study*. New York: Greenwood Press, 1988.

Walker, Margaret Urban, ed. *Mother Time: Women, Aging and Ethics*, Lanham, Md.: Rowman and Littlefield Publishers, Inc., 1999.

Walters, James W., ed. *Choosing Who's To Live: Ethics and Aging.* Urbana: University of Illinois Press, 1996.

Wei-Ming, Tu. "The Confucian Perception of Adulthood," in *Adulthood: Essays,* Edited by Erik H. Erikson. New York: Norton, 1978.

Wilson, Emily Herring. *Hope and Dignity: Older Black Women of the South*. Philadelphia: Temple University Press, 1983.

Woodward, Kathleen. *Aging and Its Discontents: Freud and Other Fictions.* Bloomington: Indiana University Press, 1991.

____, ed. *Figuring Age: Women, Bodies, Generations.* Bloomington: Indiana University Press, 1998.

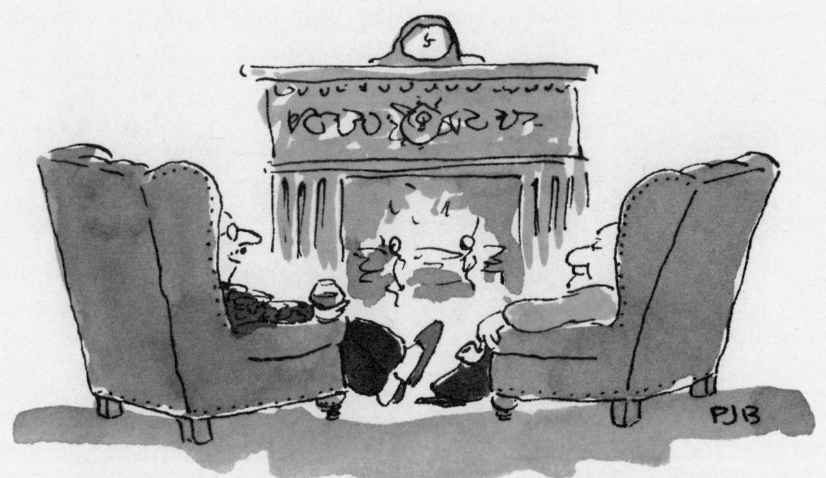

"I'm not worrying. I've got most of my money in handbaskets."

Contributors

ANNE BARLOW joined the New Museum of Contemporary Art as Curator of Education in January 1999. From 1994 to 1998 she was Curator of Modern Art and Design at Glasgow Museums in Scotland, where she played a key role in the development of the city's Gallery of Modern Art. She initiated and managed a wide range of commissions, artist residencies, new technology projects, outreach programs and exhibitions including *Pierre et Gilles: Grit and Glitter* and *Out of the Blue: Faisal Abdu'Allah, Sher Rajah and Zineb Sedira*. From 1989 to 1994 she worked as Curator of the Scottish Arts Council's collection of contemporary art, acting as chair of the purchasing committee and managing the collection's outreach scheme. Her first post after graduating with a Masters in the History of Art from Glasgow University in 1986 was with Fischer Fine Art Ltd., London.

XOCHITL DORSEY received her Master of Arts in 1999 from New York University in Latin American/Caribbean Studies and Museum Studies. She worked as an intern at the New Museum from 1998–99 assisting in the coordination of the Visible Knowledge Program projects and their integration into the exhibition. She is the recipient of a 1998–99 Foreign Language Area Studies grant and a graduate assistantship in NYU's Center for Latin American and Caribbean Studies program. She co-coordinated Istorias, a contemporary Latin American film series at NYU. She has worked as a co-editor for various university organization newsletters and has participated actively in a variety of student organizations.

ANNE ELLEGOOD joined the New Museum of Contemporary Art as a Curatorial Associate in June of 1998. From 1993 to 1997, she worked on a variety of exhibitions as a curatorial assistant and registrar for McDaris Exhibit Group, an independent traveling exhibition group. She graduated from Bard College's Center for Curatorial Studies in May of 1997 where her thesis exhibition, *Unbearable Laughter*, included the work of Nicole Eisenman, Kara Walker, and Sue Williams. Most recently, she organized a section of the 1999 David Wojnarowicz retrospective at the New Museum on the artist's activism and installed a selection of his works in the windows of Saks Fifth Avenue as part of their "Project Art" series.

PHILIP KOPLIN is a freelance science editor and self-taught artist who has had solo shows in New York and Santa Barbara. He was a co-curator of *Signs of Age: Representing the Older Body* which was presented at the Santa Barbara Contemporary Arts Forum from November 8, 1997 to January 18, 1998. He is presently working on an exhibition exploring mourning, particularly in regard to its function in defining the self-identity of the survivor(s).

MARCIA TUCKER is Founding Director of the New Museum of Contemporary Art, an institution devoted to the advancement of innovative art and artistic practice as a vital social force. Prior to founding the New Museum, Ms. Tucker was Curator of Painting and Sculpture at the Whitney Museum of American Art from 1969 to 1977. As Director of the New Museum, which was established in 1977, Ms. Tucker organized such major exhibitions as *"Bad" Painting* (1978), *Choices: Making an Art of Everyday Life* (1986), *Pat Steir* (1987), *Markus Raetz* (1988), *Bad Girls* (1994), and *A Labor of Love* (1996), among others. Abroad, she organized *The 1970s: New American Painting* for the U.S.I.A., an exhibition that toured Eastern and Western Europe in 1980 and co-curated a retrospective exhibition by the Catalan artist Perejaume at Barcelona's Museum of Contemporary Art (1999). She was chosen as United States Commissioner for the Forty-first Venice Biennale, *Paradise Lost/ Paradise Regained: American Visions of the New Decade* (1984), and she organized *Twentieth-Century American Sculpture: A Northeast Region Exhibition* for The First Lady's Garden at The White House (1996).

She is the series editor of *Documentary Sources in Contemporary Art*, five books of theory and criticism published by the New Museum. She received an M.A. in Art History from the Institute of Fine Arts at New York University, honorary doctorate degrees from the San Francisco Art Institute (1983), and the Atlanta College of Art (1997), and was named a *Chevalier dans l'Ordre des Arts et des Lettres* by the French Ministry of Culture (1997). Ms. Tucker is the 1999 recipient of Bard College's Center for Curatorial Studies Award for Curatorial Achievement and has taught, written, lectured and published widely in America and abroad.

ANJA ZIMMERMANN is an art historian and co-organizer of the *VI. Deutsche Kunsthistorikerinnentagung (6th German Conference of Feminist Art History)* in Tübingen, Germany in 1996. She has published articles on Cindy Sherman, Zöe Leonard and Cheryl Dunye in the German journal *Frauen Kunst Wissenschaft* and an essay on deconstruction and feminism in the collection *Mythen von Autorschaft und Weiblichkeit in 20.Jahrhundert/Myths of Authorship and Femininity in the 20th Century* (Marburg: Jonas Verlag, 1997). Dividing her time between Germany and New York, she is currently completing a dissertation entitled "Scandalous Bodies—Scandalous Images: Controversies on Abject Art in the United States" at Tübingen University, Germany.

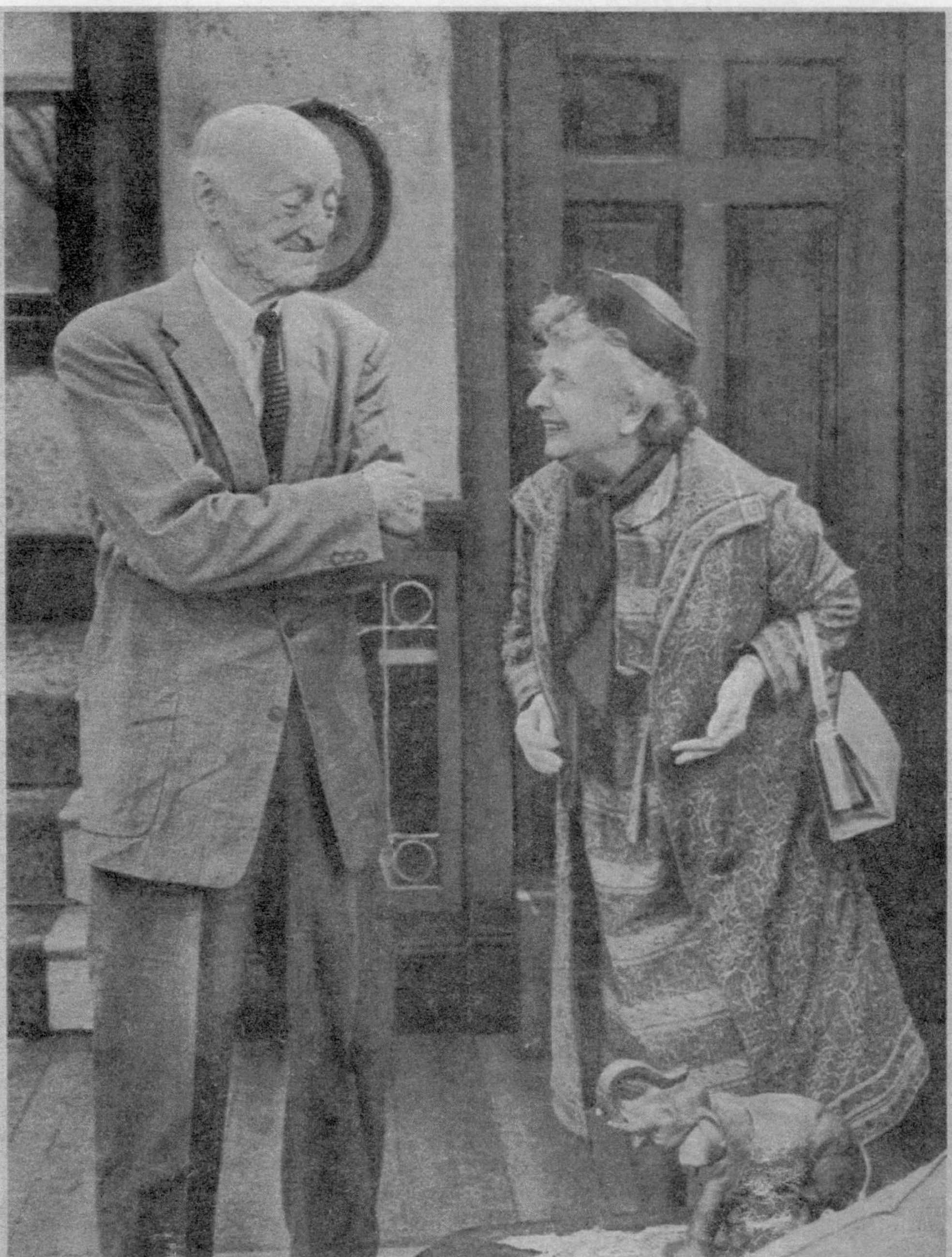
In TV's "All in the Family," Justin Quigley, played by Burt Mustin, and Jo (Ruth McDevitt) reveal to the Bunker family that they find it cheaper to live together unmarried than married.

All in the Family, *still from television program, published in* The New York Times, *January 20, 1974. In this episode, the couple reveals that they find it cheaper to live together unmarried rather than married. Burt Mustin and Ruth McDevitt, actors. With permission of Columbia TriStar Television, Los Angeles.*

New Museum Staff

Security	Kimball Augustus (57)
Curator of Education	Anne Barlow (34)
Volunteer Coordinator	Richard Barr (72)
Public Relations Coordinator	Meg Blackburn (25)
Technical Systems Manager	Kim Boatner (42)
Executive Assistant, Director's Office	Victoria Brown (32)
Installation Coordinator	Tom Brumley (34)
Senior Curator	Dan Cameron (42)
Maintainer	Raymond Caparla (26)
Membership Coordinator	Diane Carr (25)
Administrative Assistant	Deborah Cohen (31)
Admissions Clerk	Stephen Czeck (23)
Bookstore Clerk	Adam Dragon (26)
Curatorial Associate	Anne Ellegood (32)
Education Coordinator	Sarah Farsad (33)
Manager of Finance and Administration	Rika Yihua Feng (33)
Curatorial Administrator/ Publications Manager	Melanie Franklin (32)
Education Coordinator—New Media	Donna Gesualdo (30)
Registrar/Exhibitions Manager	John Hatfield (35)
Bookstore Assistant Manager	David Hunter (25)
Security	Elon Joseph (62)
Director of Operations	Patricia Kirshner (47)
Maintainer	Dwayne Langston (33)
Special Events Coordinator	Vicki Latimer (31)
Senior Sales, Bookstore	Susan Lutjen (22)
Admissions Clerk	Zulema Meijias (36)
Adjunct Curator	Gerardo Mosquera (53)
Security	Svetlana Pavlova (40)
Bookstore Clerk	Herbert Pfostl (31)
Director	Lisa Phillips (*"re-born"*)
Security	Michael Rechner (32)
Assistant Registrar	Sefa Saglam (29)
Security	Robert Santiago (34)
Grants Manager	Hasanthika Sirisena (29)
Director of Marketing and Special Events	Maureen Sullivan
Deputy Director	Dennis Szakacs (*"born free"*)
Security	Orion Taylor (33)
Founding Director	Marcia Tucker (59)
Bookstore Manager	David Tweet (35)
Accountant	David Youngwood (36)